SMART CHOICES
For
SERIOUS MONEY

How to Protect, Preserve, and Thrive In Uncertain Economic Times

By Dr. Mitch Levin, CWPP, CAPP
The Financial Physician™
Two-Time National Best Selling Author

Other books by Dr. Mitchell Levin

Power Principles for Success

Goal! The Financial Physician's Ultimate Survival Guide for the Professional Athlete

GROW—Proven Trust-Based Marketing for Financial Advisors

Payday—Your Business Sold, Now What?

Science of Successful Investing Made Simple

Shift Happens

Cover Your Assets: How to Build, Protect and Maintain Your Own Financial Fortress

Under The Radar

Table of Contents

Forward

Congratulations! That you are reading this book is a good indication that you are responsible and serious about your money. You likely made smart choices to get you to this position. Before moving forward, though, think back. Recall the last time you actually felt 100% financially free; not a financial care in the world. For most of us, it was when we were very young. For me, it was when I was around 11 years old.

Statistics and surveys show that investors are frustrated. Markets feel too risky. We are paying too much in taxes. Our rates of return are too low. Mostly written for the "middle class millionaire" (net worth between $2-20 million), in this book there also are advanced strategies outlined for the truly affluent ($20-200 million).

Though this book was written and published during the "Great Recession," and the "Great Non-Recovery," the principles throughout are universal and timeless.

This book was written to help you, whether you aspire to become or already are the middle class millionaire, or whether you are the truly affluent, regain that sense of serenity and financial freedom with more clarity, greater comfort, and solid confidence. Feel in control.

Introduction

How many of us have made financial decisions in the past that resulted in unexpected and perhaps disappointing results? Why and how did that happen? Often, this occurs because the decisions were made based upon missing information, mis-information, or myths and misconceptions -- without the knowledge of, <u>let alone the quantification of</u>, the fees, costs, expenses, taxes and the risks threatening our progress.

There is one critical question all investors should ask themselves: "If there were crucial pieces of must-know information missing from my decision making process, when would I want to know?"Today? Five years from now? Well, of course, you would want to know as soon as possible.

Many people we meet with for an initial visit are missing vital components of their decision making process, or they are not even sure how they come to their decisions. They have simply never really considered it. Each of them though, ultimately recognized the extreme hazards presented by this practice, and they are often stunned to realize they have made so many decisions without properly processing the information in a deliberate and logical way. Would you agree that this is something that might seize your attention as well?

If so, you are reading the right book. We are here to identify and address critical "must-know" facts and truths, as well as the myths, missing information, misinformation, and misconceptions, so you can make choices that are evidence-based, and rekindle your feeling of financial freedom and make great decisions.

First, let us perform simple "thought experiment." How many of us believe that we already are making decisions with complete, accurate, and clear information? If we do, then why have many of our financial results been so disappointing or, at best, unclear? Many people, prior to becoming clients, have relied upon a decision-making process that was flawed. The results were quite costly, or were silently waiting to ambush as a substantial problem in the future.

We think we are making logical, evidence-based decisions. We believe we are being good students: reading the journals, listening to the pundits, and considering all the "data." We are thoughtfully asking our accountants, our attorneys, and our brokers for their insight and for rationale. And yet statistics show that <u>investors are frustrated</u>.

Research tells us that there are hundreds of billions of dollars paid unnecessarily in phantom income tax every year. Likewise, it reveals that most people are not even aware of phantom income tax. If they have never heard of phantom income tax, how can they possibly address it, reduce it, or eliminate it? They never had an opportunity to avoid it!

More evidence supporting the "hurting investor" observation: further study tells us that market returns are typically in the eight, nine, or even ten percent range for any long-term period, according to Dalbar Research in Boston (more on this in Chapter Five). Yet investors, large and small, mom and pop, institutional, professionally managed, or "do-it-yourselfers," typically earn somewhere in the three percent range.

Where did the returns go? Another startling find comes from LIMRA, the service organization for Life Insurance Institute. Approximately three trillion dollars of annuities are purchased and 79.5% of people who own them never turn them on for income, leaving a deferred tax time-bomb for their children and families. Considering that one of the primary purposes of owning an annuity is to turn it on for income and spend it down, can we safely agree that many if not all of these people received insufficient information during their decision making process?

We know that only 50% of us have wills and trusts and that less than 50% of those are actually funded. Nor are they updated to include the necessary features and language to ensure the will work as intended. Why?

Surveys clearly reflect investor aggravation. From this research we can safely estimate that roughly 71% of financial advice-seeking clients are looking to change advisors. Many simply do not know where to turn because so many financial advisors appear to be doing the same things, in the same way, and getting the same or similar results. These surveys indicate that clients, on average, are changing financial advisors every three and a half years. We recognize this in startling contrast to our most recent analysis which reflects Summit client retention rates steadily in area of 19.6 years.

Our sincere wish is for you to enjoy this book and, hopefully, make greater progress toward full financial health. Share it with those you care about. We believe in our mission to empower each client to full financial health, understanding that this works to improve our world one investor at a time. Each of us deserves a fulfilling future; one obtained through solid growth that is safely managed, and guided by trusted advice.

Chapter 1: Begin at the Beginning

"Tell me and I forget. Teach me and I remember. Involve me and I learn."

–Benjamin Franklin

A friend and colleague of ours in Houston, Texas, Kevin Fink, came up with the Circle of Knowledge concept, and Don Blanton of MoneyTrax® incorporated this "game" into his software modules. It goes like this:

- There things we know we know (Our date of birth, social security number, and so on)
- There are things we know we do not know (How to calculate the exact speed, time, and trajectory to land an object on a distant planet, for example)
- Everything else is in our "blind spot". Such as things we know that turn out to be false (Despite two hundred years of evidence to the contrary, society, as it were, believed the earth was flat. In fact, the Flat Earth Society existed until the mid-twentieth century)
- There are also things we do not even know that we do not know.

In this book, we will share some of the things we know to be true, perhaps a few things you may not be aware of.

An Integrated Approach to Wealth Protection: "Begin with the End in Mind"

As alluded to earlier, when economic times are tough and uncertain, we have found that investors stick with their current advisors. This is not because they trust these advisors more. Rather, perhaps they believe "better the devil I know then the devil I don't." According to Bill Good in Research Magazine, these same investors are slow to make decisions, and they allow fear to outweigh the perception of opportunity. Yet, when money goes into motion, these same investors *must* make decisions. They do not have the luxury of procrastination.

In life, we face two situations where money must be put into motion: death and retirement. While in retirement, investors can procrastinate by leaving that retirement money alone, such as in their company 401(k), for example. When someone dies, money must into motion, regardless of what the market is doing. Creditors are paid, and heirs claim what is remaining, whether the market is up, down, or sideways. This will continue to be the case until people learn how to take it with them.

Interestingly, research shows that 86% of heirs who receive a substantial inheritance have plans to fire their parents' advisor. A full 79.6% fulfill this intent by changing their primary adviser after inheriting. Why is this? A primary reason is the assumption that the "old advisor" is not ready to manage the newly inherited wealth.

If you find yourself preparing your estate plan, and want to ensure that your children do not ditch your advisors in favor of someone else, you should strongly consider a fee-based, wealth preservation, and registered investment advisory firm. In addition to helping you create your wealth protection plan, a leading and comprehensive firm will take extensive measures to identify, reduce, or eliminate unnecessary fees, costs, expenses, taxes and risks that could threaten your estate. This gives you peace of mind as you prepare to leave a portion of your wealth to your family. A reliable firm will also communicate with your children and their other trusted advisors, such as their attorneys, bankers, and accountants. Creating this integrated advisor-network creates an environment of protection that is irreplaceable in terms of the sense of ease it delivers. You deserve that.

This process helps our clients avoid losses, rather than simply "trying to pick the winners" at any cost. Our approach empowers clients to preserve, protect, and grow their savings. They maintain their purchasing power, their current lifestyle, and typically rest assured in knowing they have something to pass on to their family. With the help of a firm like Summit Wealth, you can live without fear of the coming economic future.

Our objectives for wealth planning clients are:

- Establish thorough understanding of their unique circumstances, goals, concerns, and ambitions
- Develop a plan that targets their goals and needs, immediate, short and long-term, while offering the highest probability of success
- Form strong relationships with attorneys, accountants, heirs, and any other people critical to the client's financial progress, with clear communication
- Provide universal access to the most up-to-date services and tools available; easing the path to remaining informed and reliable service fulfillment
- Maintain the highest degree of transparency and disclosure possible

With these objectives met, we are able to afford our clients and their heirs the confidence derived from knowing they are in good hands and are with a team they can trust. With that confidence, they make great decisions.

Money Perspectives Matter

The heart of investing is money, so you should seek trusted advice from an investment firm who has a clearly defined and easily understandable philosophy about money. What do we know about money? The answer is plenty! We work with money for our clients and ourselves. We have studied its characteristics and capabilities, and continually apply evidence-based approaches to maximizing its power. We appreciate the importance of money and respect the impact of its absence in others' lives. This is one thrust behind Summits many philanthropic endeavors.

Yet, do we as humans truly comprehend what money is? Do we understand where it comes from, what its requirements are, or how it has changed over time? Do we realize its psychosocial implications?

Ultimately, before you begin investing, you must answer this question: "What does money mean to me?"

The truth is, money, in and of itself, is meaningless. The people who exchange it give it the power we value. In fact, it is a relatively new phenomenon, carved out of a time when the "stuff of life" was no longer manufactured or produced in our vicinity. Money became essential when we could no longer supply our own needs or depend bartering.

Money is constantly changing. Where once the dollar was backed by a gold standard, only over the last several decades has this changed. Now, money is almost entirely an intangible entity, yet our society is completely reliant upon it. Money has allowed our basic needs to become more and more intertwined and delocalized.

In some ways, money has led to less compassion in our society. Care, such as childcare, education, social work, and elder care, has been removed from the family and community and placed in institutions that require compensation. People are now being asked to stop working 30 to 40 years before they stop living, and they need money to do so. This money is typically saved, invested, or is supplied from someone else.

These are significant issues, yet we rarely talk about them. They all point to one simple fact, however: money simply signifies an agreement. It only stands for what everyone in the society collectively agrees and believes it stands for. This means it can change, and likely is. We could benefit from examining our social uses for money and how they relate to the current design and construct of money.

Money is also about the future. Money is about hope. Money is about faith. Money is about love. It is what we can do with our stored labor.

It enables us to express love by clothing, feeding, and sheltering those we care about and those who are less fortunate.

We wish to share with you some great ways to save and invest money, so you can have it to serve these social purposes and more. Then, we strive to help you put it to prudent use, so you can make great decisions.

Process vs. Product: The Canary in the Coalmine

We would only have a relationship with, and engage a firm that is a fee-based registered investment advisory firm. To understand why we take this approach, simply consider the game of golf. Professional golfers often say, "It's all about the swing; it's not about the clubs." While you do need to use the right club (and in the right way) to successfully get the ball where you want it to go, the process, or, "swing" if you will, is far more important. Once you have your process down, simply add the right club (tool, or financial product if you will), and your likelihood of success skyrockets.

You could spend hours selecting your clubs, only to fail because you hit the ball into a hazard or have a swing so wild you cannot get the ball anywhere near the green. It is the same way with investing. Financial advisors, insurance agents, annuity agents, stockbrokers and so forth are like "manufacturers reps," selling products like annuities, investments, gold, mutual funds, retirement plans, real estate, etc., and too often they declare, "Buy my (insert product here) and you will succeed!" We see it differently. We believe that the power is not in the tool; the power is in the process. Yes, deliberate success also requires integrity, strong ethics, and the expertise to determine which tool is needed, why it is needed, and the constitution to diligently monitor progress and make appropriate adjustments as needed; however, it all begins with process.

This is one reason why we believe a fee-based firm is superior. It is in the client best interest. We believe our clients should have universal access to all of the best products, or "clubs" of using the golf analogy. We believe that offering a variety of solutions on a fee-based structure gives our clients the best opportunity to achieve success in an efficient, effective and comfortable manner. They retain control, maintain their lifestyle, protect their families, and preserve their legacies as productive members of our society and community. And this fee-based structure creates a relationship wherein our success is contingent upon our client's success. We would not have it any other way.

We are not the only ones who feel this way. In the February 2012 edition of Investment News, researchers reported that finding sustainable yield for retirees has been tough in recent years. Because of this, the "four percent rule" of withdrawal (which said that if you withdraw four percent of your portfolio every year, you should not outlive your assets) has been called into question. This problem really boils down to the core of what popular-media-made investment philosophy has been during the past few years.

Chris Finefrock, Senior Analyst of ValMark in Akron, Ohio, puts it this way: in response to record low interest rates, he says, "In high volatility and equity markets, finding sustainable yield for retirees has not been an easy task. The answer to yield scarcity lies at the intersection of insurance, advisory and brokerage worlds, where independent advisors are uniquely equipped with different products and investment management tools that can work together to help generate the sustainable income and growth that retirees seek."

We believe this clearly affirms our philosophy about independent financial advisors. It's all about the process, not one particular product. That is why we offer our clients universal access to an abundance of available tools. We want to offer you everything you need to stay in control, to make informed decisions, with clear disclosure and transparency at all times.

Financial Advisors vs. Self Investing:
The Value of Professional Guidance

You may be wondering why you need a financial advisor to do what you can do yourself. This is a fair question. After all, many of us are "do-it-yourselfers." We do our own home repairs. We file our taxes. We might event attempt to handle something as complex and sensitive as a divorce.

Yet, just because we can do something does not mean that we should. There is a story about a prisoner who took out his own appendix in prison, rather than waiting for a doctor. He could do this himself, but this does not mean he should have done so.

You may think that you are capable of managing your own portfolio and personal net worth. After all, you have done a good job of amassing your wealth to this point. Yet, think about any bad investment or poor financial decision you have made. Did this mistake or misjudgment interrupt the power of compounding in your portfolio? If so, without this mistake, could your wealth be even greater? Chances are it could. We will address more about the power of compounding in a later chapter – keep this in mind as you proceed.

In investing, big mistakes can be incredibly costly. Not only that, it is quite challenging for the typical investor to keep up with the multitude of market changes. After all, you have a life and a family and perhaps a career to attend to; you may not have the time (or the tools) follow the markets as closely as effective management can require. This is why the top performers of one 10-year period of time typically become the bottom performers the following 10-year period. The market simply changes too much for the professional, let alone the average individual to keep up with it!

So why should you use a trusted advisor? Because statistics show that without one, your success is at risk. A leading advisor will identify those "must know" facts required in making great decisions. We will point out the risks, fees, costs, taxes and expenses you need to be aware of to ensure that you have a proper risk profile and realistic expectations and capabilities. Likewise, we assist you in mitigating the ever-present inflation issue, which is a common problem most self-investors run into.

Finally, and this is important, employing the expertise of a leading advisor should eliminate the impact of the "greed/fear" cycle plaguing a large amount of professional advisors, not to mention most if not all of those attempting to do it themselves. Why is this important and how is it achieved? As previously mentioned, Summit takes an evidence-based approach to investing and planning. We utilize research, not opinion, hunches, fears, excitement, ambition, rumors and the like. Adjustments are made in portfolios because well thought out, pre agreed upon thresholds are breached, triggering our disciplined system of rebalancing to take action.

The individual "do it yourselfer" has a difficult time removing the emotion from the equation – we take care of that on behalf of hundreds of our clients around the clock. Evidence and academic research trumps emotional appeal and the popular-media impulse.

Even Yale Can Fail

Not convinced that you can benefit from a financial advisor? Then take a look at what happened to Yale. Yale's David Swensen held the unofficial title of "investment genius" for many years. Yet, in 2008 when the markets crashed, his model "crashed" along with everyone else's. Mr. Swensen is a perfect example of a "do as I say, not as I do" individual, because his book on investing is excellent. It conforms perfectly with our investment philosophy, outlined in this book, which is to avoid too much risk and be prudently invested using great diversification, proper allocation, and a disciplined approach to rebalancing.

Yale's endowment, under Mr. Swensen's direction, did what so many other institutional investors did in the years prior to the crash. They started shifting money out of traditional stocks and bonds and into higher yielding alternatives, adding more risk, such as hedge funds. They also started investing in real assets like commodities, real estate, and private equity.

Their rationale was that private investments offer greater value than do the public markets; however, the private assets tend to be less inundated with capital --- less liquid. This supposedly makes them more attractive because inefficiencies are theoretically easier to find. Yes, they are also more difficult to *value*. Because they are less liquid, they are more difficult to sell and thus, realize their true value.

Even worse, there is little or no evidence to suggest that private equity or hedge fund investors have actually out-performed a properly allocated, well diversified, and diligently rebalanced portfolio. The only people who seem to do well in these funds are the fund managers themselves. By going this route, Yale lost significantly, with a drop in endowment funds from $34 billion to $27 billion. Harvard, other endowments, and public pension funds also suffered precipitous declines of other peoples' money. Had they followed the guidelines in Mr. Swensen's book, we believe they could have had much more success.

Why was this route so dangerous? The answer is clear, Yale failed to diversify sufficiently and they put their money into funds that had too much risk. Sadly, when the market crashed, these funds in the high-risk markets floundered, and they were not balanced sufficiently by lower-risk funds. This led to a huge reduction in endowment funds for the university. Were Yale an individual instead of an institution, a qualified financial advisor who offered a variety of products may have been able to prevent this mistake.

A Practical Example: Finding the Lost Money

Let us now you help stave your anxiety by helping you recapture that eroding money, the money that is unknowingly filtering out of your World of Wealth. For this we will use small, easy numbers.

Hypothetically, if you make $300,000 and you are able to save $50,000 a year, you are doing great! Of course, if you can get that extra two percent rate of return on that $50,000, you will earn $1,000 a year.

Now, if we can find and save you from losing only one percent of the erosions in the remaining $250,000 in the form of unnecessary or unknown taxation, inappropriate insurances, qualified plans, or interest payments, then that one percent on $250,000 could earn $2,500. This is a 250 % increase at no risk and no cost to you!

Case One		Case Two	
Earn	$300K	Earn	$300K
Spend	$250K	Spend	$250K
Save	$50K	Save	$50K
Extra risk/return 2%	+ $1,000/year	Extra risk/return 2%	+ $1,000/year
		Wealth Erosion Rescue (1% of $250K)	$2,500 *or* 250% increase with no added risk

We have shared this model already, but it is worth repeating. By helping find this lost money, we help maximize your investment returns. Take a macro approach to your financial life. Look at it as a whole person, a family, an entire client. Know your risk tolerances, your time horizon, and your purpose for money.

We can only help people who are willing to be open, willing to learn about things that they thought were true, yet actually are not. Are you that person?

When we find out the truth, there are only two outcomes. Either you will find out that everything is perfect and you don't need to do anything, or you will find out that things are not perfect and changes should be made. Either option is something you need to know now.

You can retire and maintain your lifestyle. You can achieve full financial health. You really can. It all starts with making great decisions.

So how does the evidence-based approach to investing work? To understand this, first we must lay some foundation. All investors have three types of money: accumulated, lifestyle, and wealth erosions. Accumulated money is the money that comes from your savings and investments. This is sometimes called the "return," and it requires you to take on some degree of risk. The second type of money is the lifestyle money, the money you require in day to day life. The third type of money is too often neglected by many financial advisors. They either do not know how to address it, or are afraid to tell you. We are talking about wealth erosions. These erosions afflict the most sophisticated investors, even those with "5 Star" CPAs. This is where you are likely losing money unknowingly and unnecessarily. We can help.

Let us examine a simple example. For round numbers, we will assume that we have someone who earns $100,000 a year and is able to save $10,000 a year. He expects to earn six percent per year, representing $600 in annual returns. He wants to earn an extra two percent on his investments, bringing his accumulated money up to $10,800. Following traditional thinking, in earning that extra two percent we will incur more… risk. On the other hand, what if after proper discovery and analysis, our team can find and stop wealth erosions in the remaining $90,000? It is immediately evident how these funds, when added to the original returns, have a tremendous impact on the overall return; with little or no added risk. Using all of the "clubs" in our bag, we would assess all money-saving opportunities, such as how (or if) he funds his mortgage, his insurance covers, retirement plan, taxes plan, and college funding strategy, to name a few. If we were to find just one percent of money being lost in the way he pays for these, he could recapture an additional $900. Now, it is as if we earned an additional nine percent. Again, how much extra risk did we take to find this money? That is correct, none. This is one example of how proper discovery and analysis can make "stretching for yield" unnecessary. Rate of return is now less important and total return is increased, often dramatically and painlessly.

Projecting forward, let us suppose this same investor thinks he can consistently earn six percent on his investments, which is not an unreasonable amount. That one percent we found is the equivalent of an additional nine percent, added to the six percent he was already going to earn. This would feel like a 15% rate of return. Not bad.

Normally, in order to get a 15% rate of return from investing alone, you would have to take on tremendous risk and stomach considerable volatility. In this hypothetical case we "earned" our imaginary investor a 15% rate of return on some of his accumulated money, with lower risk, by simply utilizing a variety of tools, as a result of our collaborative process of discovery.

That is what we do. This power is found in our process, not any one product or combination of products. The results speak for themselves.

Opportunity Cost

We may have heard and used this term. Our Readers' Digest definition is that opportunity cost is not only the money you lost to unnecessary taxes, for example, but what that lost money could have earned you over time. The compounding effect can be enormous.

Here is another hypothetical: if we select a 35 year old male who purchases a $250,000 term life insurance, with level payments for 30 years, the cost will be in the neighborhood of $1300 per year, on average. Using a six percent rate of return, the total cost then would be $157,000. A bigger expense than we may have anticipated, true; not great, yet not bad for $250,000 of death benefit. However, because it is a term policy, the policy expires after age 65. No further death benefit available.

Moreover, the $157,000 opportunity cost does not expire; it never goes away. It continues indefinitely. If we calculate to age 85, the opportunity cost is now $1.1 million. At age 100 it is over $4 million. A very big opportunity cost indeed. The power of compounding has its greatest effect in the later years. We are not advising you to refrain from buying life insurance. We are merely illustrating how significant opportunity costs are. There are better ways to buy that death benefit coverage. We will discuss that more in chapter two.

Why Seek Trusted Advice?

Over the years, we have found that those who have the most money to invest are often hesitant to trust someone to help them invest it. In a Dow Jones survey of 1,300 randomly selected U.S. investors who were at least 25 years old and had a minimum of half a million dollars to invest, 41% claimed to use online and discount brokerages to manage their own investments.

We have found this to be true. Affluent investors are often uneasy about the future, yet they are inclined to participate in do-it-yourself investing. We believe this response contributes to frustration among affluent investors who might find much greater success by using a leading wealth advisor. Only 31% use a full service firm for their investments, with only 28% turning to an independent firm.

This is unfortunate. Those who opt to have financial help are usually thrilled with the help they receive. A full 70% on the survey reported being "extremely" or "very" satisfied with the relationship they had with their advisors. Still, many refuse to get professional help.

Another way to look at this issue is through the medical lens. Consider someone who has a medical concern. While they might turn to the internet to research their possible conditions, and maybe even try to make a self-diagnosis, they will visit the appropriate medical professional when it comes to treatment.

Your money is no different. While there are a multitude of resources online, and the web can be a useful tool to teach you about investments, risk and returns, when you are ready to make a decision, you are best suited with the assistance of a highly qualified, independent, fee-based, financial professional.

We do not view online investment opportunities as a threat. In fact, when used properly, one can achieve some degree of success. What we do view as a threat, however, is human behavior. The average individual, no matter how affluent he or she may be, tends to panic in bear markets or get greedy in a bull market. While these are natural emotions shared by all, they are a major contributor to poor and unpredictable performance attained by the average do-it-yourself investor.

Many affluent know this. In another survey, 1,000 millionaires were questioned, and 42% said they did not feel wealthy. When asked what would make them feel that way, they typically answered "seven-and-a-half million dollars worth of assets to invest." Four out of 10 responded that their biggest fear was not having enough income to support their current lifestyle when they retired. A full 64% were worried about the potential tax changes that could affect their investments and retirement savings.

These worries are well founded. Taxes can, and often do, increase, especially when investors are in the upper tax brackets. Investments can, and do, fail. This is why working with a financial advisor is so important. We understand taxes, inflation, costs, fees and investment behavior, and we can help you navigate all of them to make evidence based decisions.

We also strive to offer you all of the tools you need for a thorough discovery process. This allows you to take an evidence-based, logical approach to assessing your current situation, outlining your path to your goals, and implementing your plan to achieve them. In the end, we believe you should have a full set of tools (like a full set of golf clubs. If you were playing golf, you ought to know how to swing a club, which to club to swing and why. And you cannot play the game without the clubs) for you to use along with your thorough understanding of the process at hand.

Key Takeaways

- Begin with the end in mind
- Work with a "Fee Based" firm
- Connect your trusted advisors
- Focus on Process, *not* products
- Understand the impact of "opportunity cost"

Chapter 2: Find the Money at No Risk

"Plans are nothing; planning is everything."

–Dwight D. Eisenhower

The Evidence-based Way

You will read or hear time and time again that the foundation of our philosophy is to provide you with the knowledge you need to make good decisions. The repetition is worth it. One of the first ways we do this – using a thorough and simple discovery process – is by clearly outlining our philosophy for you, so you can know who we are and how we approach money, investments and wealth planning.

Team Philosophy

Have you ever been so passionate about something that you made it your mission? Well, it is our mission to empower full financial health. Our focus is primarily on the process, rather than the product. We believe that by focusing on the process, and then prudently applying that process, we are ultimately led to the appropriate tool or product. To aid in that endeavor, we take a strong team approach.

We have carefully assembled a dedicated team of experts, and we function as a unit throughout our organization. When we bring in a new client, together we discuss the client's goals, fears, ambitions, challenges, and resources. With all aspects reviewed, we can best apply our process to provide the client with exactly what he or she needs and wants.

Like the Mayo or Cleveland Clinic has a team of specialists, each member of our team has his or her own area of expertise. Remember, eye surgery was my first career. We had a team of experts in the operating with us. We work together, because none of us can do alone what all of us can do together.

The team approach renders more effective and efficient service and ensures any and all "financial blind spots" are removed. As a result, our employees are happy not only with their career, but also with their workplace. We have a motto that when somebody comes to work for our firm, we want this to be the last place they'll ever work.

Trust: The Critical Factor

Most of us have heard the saying, "Trust comes on foot and leaves on horseback." This reflects how important the trust building process is and it clearly illustrates the respect that trust demands. Once trust has been destroyed, it is virtually impossible to regain. In these uncertain times, we can appreciate the high value placed on trust and accept the challenges incurred in working to gain it. We get it – we see it the same way.

We have the privilege of working in an industry in which we can provide tremendous guidance and service to clients, families, organizations, and institutions. The impact of much of our work will literally span generations. However, the media would have us believe that "bad guys" abound in this very same industry. Considering more than 600,000 financial advisors in the United States, two names stand out from the crowd: Ponzi and Madoff. When headlines about their scandalous behavior hit the press, it gave firms across the country a bad name. The consequences of their behavior gave our honorable discipline a black eye. As you can imagine, this is deeply disturbing.

There are approximately 50 others who have either been convicted or accused of fraud from as little as $330,000, all the way up to the $50 billion range. They are found across the nation and work for all types of companies. Individuals like these make it difficult for true fiduciaries like us to gain your trust. This is a big reason why we value it so much and, once attained, we respect it, protect it, and honor with each decision, recommendation, and action we face.

As a federally registered investment advisory firm, a "fiduciary" elects to place ourselves in a position where we are ethically, morally, and legally obligated to put our clients' interest ahead of our own. We understand that our fiduciary role alone is not enough to earn your trust. We believe there are many avenues to cultivating trust.

Your confidentiality should be held in the highest regard. Your advisor should never take possession of your funds. You should have access to your accounts and account information, 24 hours a day, seven days a week. A leading wealth advisor should simply direct you and your accounts, with the guidance of your mutually agreed upon Investment Policy Statement.

Fiduciary (Summit Wealth)	Broker (Traditional)
Wealth Advisors	Sales People
Independent (Fee Based)	Biased (Commission Driven)
Comprehensive	Selective
Academic Research	Marketing Research
Prudently Built and Managed Portfolios	Portfolios Profitable to Business
Fiduciary Responsibility to Client	Responsibility to Business Bottom Line
Success Linked to Client Success	Success Linked to Own Success

Our client relationships are, like many others types of relationships, built upon trust. Many people try to "gain a client to make a sale;" however, we believe in developing solutions to gain a client. As we have mentioned, average duration a client stays with a financial services firm is roughly 3 ½ years. We believe our long-term development of trust is a significant contributor to our client retention rate more than quadrupling industry average. Your advisor should not just say more, they should do more, and do it consistently.

We typically advise our clients on all of their assets and on all of their major financial decisions using our process-based approach. We first build trust by listening well, and the quality of our response reflects this. The trust is perpetuated by how attuned our recommendations are to your goals, hopes, concerns, limitations, and opportunities. Finally, the quality of our implementation, monitoring, managing, and progress reporting and communications keeps clients informed and sleeping well at night.

The fiduciary model is a terrific method of gaining and maintaining trust. In placing our client's interests ahead of our own, we exceed industry standards of suitability by a long shot. We work for you; we don't work for any company. We get paid by you; we don't get paid by any company. As your account grows, we prosper. As your account declines, we suffer.

Longevity is a serious consideration in this business. Similar to our investment perspective, our business management is long-term. We just recently completed our 10-year business plan and are working on a 30-year plan. We have considered a 70-year plan. Why? The first reason is that we have young clients, some under 30, who are going to live another 70 years. Additionally, our clients' families should have confidence that the great advice and service they receive today will be available for years to come. Therefore, we have an obligation to be certain that our purpose, our process, our philosophy and our people are intact for the long-term. We are working to make the world better one investor at a time, and this requires long- term planning.

We are on a mission to empower you to full financial health. Too many of our colleagues and friends and family members have suffered. And if a $13 Billion Foundation underperforms, what chance can the rest of us have. That is why we took matters into our own hands. We are and should be in the long-term relationship business. Because you did not amass your wealth over night. And you do not want to last a short period of time. It requires tobe vigilant and diligent on your behalf for your lifetime, and beyond.

Trust is the only thing we offer. It is the reason so many of our clients remain clients so long. It is the only reason so many attorneys, accountants and other professionals introduce us to their clients. It is the reason so many hundreds of millions are attracted and entrusted to us.

As you can see, we are passionate about the trust we have built with our clients. We guard it carefully and jealously to ensure it is never infringed upon or degraded. We hold our team accountable, not only to you, but also to ourselves, to be certain that we're continuing to honor that trusted position. In fact, our unique value proposition embodies it – solid growth, safely managed, trusted advice. Together, those initiatives work to secure your better future.

Blocking and Tackling

Many things can threaten the lifestyle you have worked hard to create: death, taxes, inflations, disability, unexpected life events, lawsuits, births, divorce, and even technological changes. While many of these events are unavoidable, much can be done to ensure their impact is minor modification, rather than a catastrophic nightmare. You should seek the help of experts who can understand, identify, and then reduce, solve, or even eliminate those threats to your current and future lifestyle. This affords the one thing that money alone cannot buy: security.

Prudent planners focus on preparing, rather than repairing. If we can help you avoid losses, rather than helping you rebound from them, we have succeeded. This strategy is more powerful than "picking the winners." We believe that being consistently excellent outperforms occasional brilliance. We believe we can remove, reduce, or mitigate those threats, and potentially avoid them or eliminate them altogether at times. The premise is simple: we cannot control the wind, but we can adjust our sails.

Once your threats are addressed, we can shift attention to your opportunities. Too many in our industry try to focus on the opportunities first, ignoring the threats. They ignore the costs, the fees, the expenses, the taxes and the risks. The industry is continually introducing new products, and these products often have problems and are quite risky if applied without in-depth and comprehensive analysis. Yet we (consumers) are encouraged to buy them through marketing efforts that relay only the possible benefits, while undisclosed threats exist.

Opportunity-first type planning can work well for some people, but it has some serious flaws; some particularly for significant wealthy individuals. First, this type of planning is "needs based." For instance, this approach often assumes a lower tax bracket in retirement. It assumes that traditional retirement plans (including government plans, such as IRAs, 401(k)s and qualified plans), equal tax implications. In some ways, it implies that by simply increasing your rate of return you will increase your wealth. A common behavior under this assumption is the practice of chasing returns, rather than reducing risk.

Sadly, many financial professionals who focus on a opportunity-first planning model minimize the effects of inflation, cost of living, and decreasing purchasing power – all of which affect investors into and through retirement. With our philosophy of avoiding risks, we are always cognizant of problems like these that could derail our clients' financial goals in the future. Likewise, strive to empower our clients with the tools to avoid them or plan for them accordingly.

A fundamental objective of our firm is the dutiful transfer of our knowledge. Knowledge leads to wisdom, and ultimately, wise choices. Wisdom combined with compassion helps combat arrogance. Because we provide knowledge and wisdom with compassion, we are able to offer trusted advice to our clients. Combine this trusted advice with solid growth that is safely managed, and you are ready to make great decisions.

Defining a Top Advisor

A top firm approaches the recruitment of advisors and all supporting staff with tremendous prudence. We seek to employ the industry's best and we are pleased with the team we have assembled. As we look to add advisors to our team, we look for those that are clearly top advisors by meeting these seven specific criteria:

1. Focus on Process, Not Product

One of the first ways we identify a top investor is by finding someone who believes in our process-based approach. When an advisor agrees that "it is the process, not the product," they could be a good fit for our team.

2. Careful Client Selection

A second characteristic of a top advisor is someone who specializes and knows that not everyone they meet will be suitable for Summit. Many advisors believe they must accept every piece of business that comes their way; however, a top advisor focuses on the ideal client, putting all of their resources into finding and then helping the candidates they can most effectively serve and bring value to. Our team is careful when extending a Summit relationship to qualified consumers. We want to work with people who find our approach and our solutions rational and beneficial.

3. System Driven

The third characteristic is someone who can systematize processes and solutions. Top advisors are systematic. They know that exceptions breed inefficiencies. A considerable amount of effort goes into developing their solutions, and thus they expect their clients to implement their solutions. Clients are typically eager to do so, because the advice helps them reach their financial goals.

4. Utilize Multiple Communication Funnels

Top advisors utilize varying communication channels. They recognize the value of gaining exposure through educational seminars, radio programs, through a tax practice, and many other avenues. By utilizing multiple platforms, top advisors attract new relationships, as well as great visibility within the community.

5. Time is Precious

Top advisors value their time. To understand this, it is easier to consider the opposite. Advisors who are not at the top of their game clearly illustrate a lack of value for their time. Top advisors do not have the luxury of extra time, because they are busy helping their clients. Top advisors make you feel as though you are the most important person in the room, because that is what you are and that is what you deserve.

6. Avoid "Shiny Object Syndrome"

Many advisors are notorious for having "shiny object syndrome." In other words, they are product driven or marketing driven and end up chasing after the next "attractive" option. Top advisors know very specifically what their value is and they do not get distracted. Instead, they put on their blinders and focus on serving their clients. You do not typically find them chasing fads. They know what works, and they keep doing it successfully time and time again. Remember, consistent excellence rather than occasional brilliance.

7. Easily Understood

Top advisors avoid industry jargon. At Summit Wealth, we believe in giving each of our clients the knowledge they need to make great decisions, but that cannot happen if we are throwing fancy industry terms at them all the time. We strive to present complex ideas in clear, understandable ways. They do not rely upon flashy PowerPoint presentations to help their clients understand their options. In simple, concise terms, they explain what their clients need to know.

So, to sum it up, how can you identify a top advisor? Look for these seen characteristics:

1. Focus on Process, Not product
2. Careful Client Selection
3. System Driven
4. Utilize Multiple Communication Funnels
5. Time is Precious
6. Avoid "Shiny Object Syndrome"
7. Easily Understood

A well educated and experienced team of Senior Wealth Advisors can and should perform a True Market Investment Analysis (TMIA--more on this in later chapters) for you. The TMIA examines your portfolio's efficiency, producing a cost analysis of how you are really doing, and then provides an overlap study revealing opportunities for improvement.

Why should you ask for the True Market Investment Analysis? By working with a team of trusted expert specialists, you have only two possible outcomes, and they are both great. First, you may learn that you are doing everything well. This provides peace of mind and encouragement to continue doing what you are doing. Second, you could learn what you are doing that is costing you. Wouldn't you want to know that right now? Get the information, knowledge, wisdom, and trusted advice you need to ensure your better future.

How We View Investor Behavior

Money Attitudes Matter

Most people have a very emotional attitude toward money, and this can cause them to make investment mistakes. One of the ways we help our clients is by helping them understand and manage their attitudes toward money.

Money, and how you view it, is all a matter of perspective. For instance, if someone holds up a glass of orange juice and asks you what it is, you may say, "It is a glass." It is only a glass if someone drinks from it. If they use it to hold down papers on their desk when the window is open, it is a paperweight. If they throw it at someone else, it becomes a weapon; it is all in your matter of perspective.

Consider someone who has two oranges. If he places those two oranges on the countertop, they are still two oranges. Adding two more makes it four oranges, but they are still oranges. Coming back the next day does not change anything. Coming back in a month changes much in the freshness of the fruit, but they are still oranges. Waiting 20 or even 40 years, however, changes them into a pile of dust or a mere stain. Those oranges were impacted by outside forces, and they have changed. The only reason they changed, however, was because of those outside forces.

Money is a lot like these two scenarios. On one hand, it is defined by how it is used. It can be "income," an "investment," or something else, depending on how it is used.

However, what it is at its most fundamental level does not change, except through outside forces, such as fees, costs, taxes, risks, and inflation. Over a long period of time, that money can get eroded away, much like the oranges, but only through outside influences. What we want for our clients is the ability to understand this, then to make decisions to ensure that they do not come in on fumes, can maintain their lifestyles, protect their families, preserve their communities,and leave a little behind when all is said and done.

In the end, money is a tool, something to be used, not something to feel emotional about. When we are successful in helping remove the emotion from your relationship with money, then we can help you set up a plan to protect, preserve and even grow the money you have.

One aspect that consistently impacts investor success is investor behavior. Our team works as hard as possible to help clients succeed, yet in the end, we can only do so much. Ultimately, it is up to you, as our client, to make the final decisions. Our goal is to provide you with accurate information so you can make wise decisions; however, the ultimate decision comes down to you.

Think for a moment about the worst investment you have ever made. What was it? How much did you lose? Who told you about it?Think about your overall investment performance. If we are truthful with ourselves, we are all somewhat frustrated as investors. This is reflected in the fact that most investors stay with their advisors on an average of a mere three and a half years. Surveys also point to this frustration. Despite the fact that most clients are smart, sophisticated, and logical, many are making financial decisions without knowing the specific questions to ask or which pieces of information they are missing.

Some people are happy to give their investments over to "their guy" and walk away. Yet, there are issues that, if you've never heard of them, will quickly derail your investment success.Take, for example, phantom income tax. Phantom Income Tax occurs when you have taken a loss in principal, yet still owe a tax. Say you have a building that is now worth $1 million. You may have paid $1.4 million several years ago. Fortunately, you collect $70,000 per year in rent. Well, you now owe tax on the rental income, while you have suffered a loss of $400,000.

This happens in mutual funds even more frequently, and more

insidiously. For example, the fund manager has caused you a Net Asset Value loss, at least on paper until you sell the fund. Yet during the year, that manager was able to sell more winners than losers to offset the overall loss of value. A perfect example is someone who had a good portfolio of $2 million. The portfolio was down only 7%. That in and of itself is not too bad, relatively speaking, right? Of course, that translates into a $140,000 loss. Now it seems worse. It gets even worse. The fund manager, in the course of managing the portfolio, selling more winners than losers, caused the investor to receive a 1099 from the IRS for over $85,000. The investor had to pay $30,000 in tax.

Imagine how you would feel if that were you having to write the check to the IRS for experiencing a loss in your investments. The indignity of throwing good money after bad. Yet it happens all the time, until we can fix the situation.

If you have never heard about this, how can you address it, reduce it, eliminate it, or avoid it altogether. We know that there are hundreds of billions of dollars paid in taxes unnecessarily to the IRS through phantom income tax, yet most advisors and their clients do little to avoid or stop it. We believe you can and should take steps to stop this unnecessary expense. You simply just need the information and insight – all of it.

Another example of this problem of trusting an advisor with insufficient information is the $3 trillion worth of deferred annuities. We have a situation where there is a tremendous amount of money tied up in annuities, yet only 79.5% of the accounts are actually "turned on" for income. This leaves an enormous tax time-bomb for beneficiaries.

Another problem that clients often do not realize exists is the trillions and trillions of dollars stuck in retirement accounts, where losses and fees eat away at returns. Often, people take their required minimum distributions, even though they do not need that money, and leave a tax nightmare for their beneficiaries. This type of investor behavior inadvertently harms your future goals for your money.

The Dalbar Study illustrates another example of this type of money being lost due to misunderstandings, misconceptions, or missing facts. The study shows that over any 20-year period of time, investors tend to under perform significantly due to fees, costs, or taxes that were not identified or quantified. This led to an uncomfortable risk exposure and losses now or in the future.

Why are these mistakes being made? It is not because investors are reckless with their money. This indicates insufficient discovery was performed. There is very often a flaw in investor's decision making process (see the Introduction). Advisors often fail to take a complete look at the client's financial profile and future goals, and thus do not address these issues.

We believe that a thorough discovery process is essential when meeting with a new prospective client. Only by implementing Summit's in-depth discovery process can all aspects be analyzed, all questions answered, inefficiencies exposed, and a path to corrective action be developed. This simply cannot occur by surface level interviews or shallow questionnaires. The terrific thing is, this discovery process is easily accomplished and understood, does not cost a dime, and always produces results. No brainer.

Another investor behavior factor is motivation. Behavioral finance professors have identified at least four investment behaviors that are not as purely rational as we would like to believe. Because of these behaviors, investors often make counterproductive decisions and end up creating the bad outcome they are trying to avoid. These behaviors are:

- *The Disposition Effect* – Selling profitable holdings too early and unprofitable ones too late
- *Overconfidence* – The belief that you can outperform the market consistently, reliably, and predictably.
- *The Endowment Effect* – Placing more value on things you own simply because you own them and you have become emotionally attached to them.
- *Anchoring* – When a client becomes fixated on one piece of data,

even though the information is outdated. They may say something like this: "If I'd paid $80 for a stock that's now under $70, I wouldn't sell it until it gets back to $80 because that's my anchor."

The solution to managing these behaviors and achieving improved results is identifying someone you trust who is process driven, uses evidence and research to form decisions – not trends, rumors, hunches, or tricks. They should be willing to examine your complete financial picture, not just the areas they can profit from, and they should have the expertise to educate you regarding your threats, opportunities, and paths to success. They should also consistently illustrate the quality of their listening through how they communicate back to you. You should feel understood; nothing less.

Studies have shown again and again that the dominant determinate of real life, long-term investment outcomes is not investment performance; it is investor behavior. We care more about where you are and where you are going than where the markets are and where they are going.

We have no control over the markets, the economy, taxes, or inflation. We do, however, have control over how we respond to them, anticipate them, and manage them.

The biggest misconception among today's investors is the idea that "I've got it taken care of." Sadly, the data shows otherwise. Finding these risks and losses and helping you make informed decisions, rather than emotional ones, is our job. With our help, investors begin to let go of these negative behaviors, identify and stop unnecessary losses, and achieve greater success.

Key Takeaways
- The team approach is optimal
- Trust is the most critical factor
- Fiduciary = Advisor works for client, not a company
- Focus on preparing, rather than repairing
- Beware of *phantom income tax*

Chapter 3: Protect Your Nest Egg

"Someone's sitting in the shade today because someone planted a tree a long time ago."

–Warren Buffet

You might have heard the saying: if you find yourself in a hole, first stop digging. Avoiding the losses is more powerful than trying to pick the winners. Avoiding the losses is the first step in stopping the "digging." Our primary objective is to protect our clients from unnecessary risks and common (and costly) investing mistakes. We work to provide accurate information so you can make great decisions and have realistic expectations – always and everywhere.

Protecting You from Tax Scams

Handing over your financial documents to a tax preparer and hoping they do a good, honest job for you can be a scary proposition. That individual needs to be well trusted, because they will hold all of your financial and personal information. Not only that, they have the potential to help you file as efficiently as possible or hand you a significant tax bill.

Sadly, fraudsters commonly commit scams during tax season. Identity theft, phishing, and intentional return preparation errors are all common. We help protect clients from these whenever possible. Identity theft is one of the more common scams. This occurs when someone uses your personal information for their own personal gain.

One in every 10 consumers in the United States has been victimized by identity theft, and this accounted for a loss of $31 billion in 2008 alone.

You can avoid identity theft by keeping your Social Security information safe and secure. Check your credit report at least once a year from sites like Experian, TransUnion, or Equifax. Be careful regarding how much personal information, such as your birthday, is made public on social media sites. If you think your identity has been stolen, file an affidavit with the Internal Revenue Service.

Phishing refers to a situation where fraudsters "fish" for your information by sending an email that appears legitimate, urging you to fill out important personal information by clicking on a link or attachment. This may look like it comes from your bank or, worse, the IRS. Remember, your bank will rarely initiate contact with you via email, and the IRS never will.

You can avoid these scans by being very cautious about emails you receive. Look for grammatical and spelling errors in emails, which are rare from government entities and large financial institutions that have the funds to pay professional writers. Never click on links or attachments that come in an email unless you are certain it's safe, and avoid giving your information over the phone if someone calls you. If you get an email that seems legitimate, always contact the organization directly before acting on the information contained in the email to ensure that the communication you receive is, in fact, legitimate.

Return preparation fraud occurs when you give your tax return to someone else to prepare, and they charge unethically for their services. Stay away from preparers that charge a percent of your return. These professionals should charge by the job or by the hour. Choose your preparer carefully, checking with the Better Business Bureau to ensure that they have good ratings. Look for preparers that have a Preparer Tax Identification Number (PTIN), a number all legitimate prepares will carry.

Anyone is able to fall victim to a scam, but the elderly and low income individuals appear to be specifically vulnerable. If you feel you have been the victim of a tax scam, contact the IRS immediately. Those who are caught committing tax fraud could spend up to five years in prison and be forced to pay restitution.

Each day we help clients make smarter financial decisions. Avoiding tax fraud is one way we do this. We apply a disciplined, methodical, rigorous, and systematic approach to each situation to help clients achieve long-term success and make great decisions.

Protecting You from the Government Deficit

The government's deficit is a very real problem that has the potential to impact your investment and wealth planning efforts. At Summit Wealth, we want you to understand the reality of the deficit and how it could impact you. Is the deficit worse than we think? Is the government using fuzzy, scary, or inaccurate arithmetic? These are valid questions that deserve answers.

If you figure in the unfounded or underfunded commitments to Social Security participants, Medicare patients, pensions, and healthcare for government retirees, plus retirement and disability payments for the military, the government's debt increased by $5.3 trillion in 2010. The future debt was $62 trillion at the beginning of 2010, according to USA Today. That is more than four times the official debt ceiling of $14.3 trillion.

Yet, if you review USDebtClock.org, that number is much closer to $100 trillion. There are currently 311 million people in the country, only 111 million of whom are tax payers. These numbers mean that every taxpayer in the country "owes" more than $1 million.

This seems pretty straightforward, and also a little scary, yet sadly it is not as cut and dried as the numbers seem to indicate. There is an obvious flaw in this type of analysis, as it counts future entitlements and pension payments as government obligations, ultimately becoming the obligations of private households, but not as assets of the people who benefit.

For instance, if a government retiree who is entitled to a pension of $35,000 a year takes that benefit, the money becomes both a cost to the government and taxpayers, as well as a benefit to the retiree. In the debt analysis, only the cost is taken into account, not the benefit.

And that is not the only flaw. For the most part, these sorts of approaches assume that a dollar is a dollar no matter when it comes in or goes out. Yet, we all know that a dollar tomorrow is worth a lot more than it will be 50 years from now due to the effects of inflation. A dollar today can be invested at five percent and be worth $11.46 in 50 years. Yet if you hold that same dollar and do not invest it, in that same 50 years, this time considering a five percent discount, it is only worth a meager eight cents. Much of the $100 trillion that the government supposedly owes is in dollars decades from now.

Pointing out these logical flaws does not lessen how serious the deficit or debt is. This is a serious problem. It is real and it puts our republic at risk; however, it may not be as bad as we think. On the other hand, it could be a lot worse than we think. Normalizing interest rates would raise the debt service cost by $4.9 trillion over 10 years, dwarfing any savings from the budget cuts currently on the floor.

We all know that only serious long-term spending reduction in the entitlement area can begin to address the nation's deficit and debt problems. We know there is no way to raise taxes enough to cover these problems. If we were to tax 100% of the income earned by those making more than $250,000, and we tax 100% of all corporate profits in America, that's still only enough money to fund the government through about 9 ½ months of the year. Clearly, raising taxes alone is not going to be the answer to the debt and deficit problem.

Yet, all of this talk is showing just how little any of us know about what is going on. Analyzing the situation is very difficult because of the assumptions being made in growth rates of the economy, assumptions made on inflation, assumptions made on interest rate changes, and assumptions made on investments. Truthfully, nobody knows what's going to happen, but we do know we cannot continue as we are. Summit Wealth strives to protect clients from the deficit by helping them prepare for all eventualities so they, in turn, can make great decisions.

Protecting Against Social Security Tweaking

Are you relying on Social Security? Chances are you already are aware that this is not a good idea, yet you have worked for the money in your Social Security funds, and you have a right to expect them to be there. Yet, they may not be available quite as you expect.

Congress has a very real problem on its hands with the budget deficit. With the national debt continuing to increase, they have to find a way to balance the budget to stop the bleeding. Yet, one side of the fence is completely opposed to cutting spending, while the other side is complete opposed to raising taxes, so no real solution exists.

Warren Buffet in a recent interview put it quite well. He found a way to help balance the budget quickly. If Congress does not balance the budget by the time re-election rolls around, then no member of Congress could be eligible to run for re-election.

Sounds like a good idea, right? While we all might agree that this particular solution makes sense, it's not likely to happen. Instead, Congress often resorts to tweaking the benefits they have promised people, and this is an option we watch carefully as it can directly affect our clients. After all, Social Security is one area that government looks to tweak.

See, directly cutting Social Security would destroy any Congress member's chances of re-election. So, instead, they change the formula that determines how the benefits increase over time. They slow the increase in Social Security and other government benefit programs, including federal pensions, to try to balance the budget and address the long-term financial problem of Social Security. This change slows the increase of government spending across various programs, while also boosting tax collection.

How does this work? Social Security payments, along with other federal benefits, are adjusted annually to keep pace with inflation, as determined by the Labor Department's consumer-price index, or CPI. The CPI measures the average change in the price for a fixed basket of goods and services. However, the CPI does not account for the change in consumer's shopping habits.

For example, if the price of chicken goes up, then the consumer may buy steak instead. The inflation measurement that takes these changes into account is the chain-weighted CPI. This, as you can imagine, generally rises slower than the main CPI benchmark.

If Congress goes by the chain-weighted CPI, this brings smaller increases in your Social Security benefits. And, since increase in the standard deduction and tax brackets are also set to the measurement of inflation, changing the chain-weighted CPI, and thus having a slower increase, results in more taxable income.

While we cannot predict what Congress will do, we can look at past behavior to show that they will likely try to adjust the Social Security formula for their advantage. We strive to protect our clients from this by providing them with solid information if and when these changes occur. With the right information, you can make the right decisions.

Protecting You from Mortgage Risk

Have you been working hard to pay your house off early? Did you know that doing so actually carries some risk? Remember equity in the house doesn't earn anything. When you have equity, you have no liquidity, use, or control of that money. In other words, the funds are difficult to tap into should you need them. Sure, you have a large, hopefully valuable asset, yet you can do little with it.

Let us consider an example. Say we have a client named Dr. Affluent who has a million dollar house and put $300,000 down when he bought it. He has been rapidly paying it off because he wants it paid off in 10 years rather than 30. So, he is been adding to his monthly mortgage payments to frontload the loan.

At some point in this process, he decides he wants to take a missionary trip and provide surgeries to the indigent population in a remote corner of the world. He is going to take his family, and he will be away for three months. While he is away, he misses his June and July mortgage payments. He figures he is safe because he has been paying ahead and has dropped his mortgage balance-owed from $700,000 to $350,000. That should count for something, right? Not exactly.

On a 30-year note, the mortgage holder pays the mortgage 12 months out of the year, equaling 360 payments. By paying ahead, he's been able take the extra payment and deduct it from the end of these 360 payments. In other words, he made payment number 360, then number 359, then number 358. Until he reaches those final payments, he is still required to make the minimum payment each month.

Now, there is a little known rule that allows a mortgage holder to file foreclosure proceedings after the borrower missed payments for 91 days. Missing three payments in a row, or technically, two payments and 31 days, can start these proceedings. In addition, the lender is only required to sell the home for the balance on the mortgage, not for its full value.

So now, because he missed these payments, Dr. Affluent's bank can choose to foreclose. He only has a $350,000 principle balance on the mortgage of a million dollar house. Therefore, the bank only has to liquidate the house for $350,000. If they do, the mortgage will be discharged.

In this hypothetical scenario, the bank tried to contact Dr. Affluent to discuss the situation, but they could not because he was on his remote missionary trip. So they have a million dollar house they are sitting on and losing money, with no way of knowing the intensions of the borrower. In light of this, they decide to have a quick sale for $450,000. They take their $350,000 payoff, and Dr. Affluent is left with just $100,000 and no home.

Of course, this particular scenario is pretty far-fetched (yet true), but that does not mean it could not happen. The fact is, uncommon things can and do happen, especially to those who are in a high net worth category. That is why we want to protect our clients against unnecessary mortgage risk. Paying off your mortgage early can be a wise financial move, yet only if you make this move with all of the knowledge and understanding necessary to make great decisions.

Protecting You from Tax Mistakes

Over the years we have found that many advisors recommend that their clients practice tax loss harvesting. While this can be affective, we recommend a "look before you leap" approach. Tax loss harvesting is far from the no-brainer that some advisors might suggest, and this strategy can easily backfire. Steps you take to minimize your taxes today might come back to haunt you tomorrow, especially given the latest round of chaos on Capitol Hill.

Often, the true tax savings in this strategy is far smaller than people have been led to believe. Kent Smetters, a tax expert and professor of risk management at the University of Pennsylvania's Wharton School, warns that tax loss harvesting can easily end up costing you money. Here's why:

Imagine you put $10,000 into an ETF for the S&P 500 in the fall of 2007. Let's say it's now at $8,000 and you sell it immediately and put the money into some other ETF of the S&P 500. As a result, you have a $2,000 long-term capital loss on the fund that can save you hundreds of dollars in taxes on capital gains that you had elsewhere in your portfolio. If you did not lock any gains, then you can use the loss to offset your ordinary income with savings valued at $700, provided you are in the 35% federal tax bracket.

This strategy allows you to reduce your taxes today, or "harvest" your loss. This is the good news. The bad news is subtle. By doing this, you might have raised your taxes tomorrow.

Let us say that the index fund grows in value over the next decade to $16,000. Had you not sold in 2010, then a decade from now you would have a gain of $6,000 over your original $10,000 purchase price. When you sold in 2010 as an opt into a similar fund, you lowered your entry price, or tax basis, to $8,000. This means 10 years from now, you will owe taxes on an extra $2,000 in gains.

Where do we believe capital gains taxes are going? If tax rates stay constant, you will come out ahead, by a little. After accounting generously for the fact that dollars today are worth more than dollars tomorrow, Professor Smetters warns that your true tax savings would amount to a mere $77 in this scenario. And, this doesn't account for what you would have earned if you had invested the tax break back into the fund. If capital gains increase from the current 15% to what some expect to be a 39.6%, plus the 3.8% Medicare tax, we are looking at almost a 300% increase in that tax bracket.

By harvesting your losses now, you could be reducing your losses later. We are not fond of paying a tax you do not have to pay. But tax deferral is a misnomer. It should read tax "postponement". After all, that is all you are doing. The tax must get paid. And then it leads to the question of what the tax rate will be when you finally do pay the tax. By paying a tax now at a rate that you know, and is historically low, thus avoiding a tax later at a rate that you do not know, and that could be higher, might result in a very large savings indeed. And since capital gains are historically low taxes right now, we are paying a low tax now to offset the higher tax later. If there are better ways, why not take the opportunity to help protect from this potential mistake?

Tax loss harvesting is not the only potential tax-related problem you should address. We also want to make sure that you are fully aware of all potential tax breaks, and when you should or should not take advantage of them.

For example, there is a new tax break that began in 2011 and extended through 2012 for employees with a 401(k). Under this tax break, employees could transfer their 401(k) into a Roth 401(k), a move that was previously not allowed. If that is possible, we encourage you to do so if it is efficient. While you will pay income taxes on the transfer, the Roth account will then grow tax deferred with tax-free withdrawals, and there are several other benefits of this transfer as well.

This is just one example of a tax break you might not know of but could take advantage of. Another is a recent change in annuities. Right now, if you hold an annuity outside of your retirement plans, these changes allow you to draw income off part of your annuity while still allowing the rest of it to grow.

Here's how this could work, according to the American Council of Life Insurance. Consider an imaginary investor named Mary who is 65 and has invested $100,000 in a deferred annuity that now has a total current value of $150,000. She would like to draw a reliable income stream from $75,000 of this.

Beginning in 2011, Mary easily segregated $75,000 of her total assets into a separate portion that had a term of 10 or more years. At current rates, Mary would receive several hundred dollars a month for life from this annuity, and two out of three dollars paid out to her would be tax free. When she separated her $75,000, her total pot consisted of 1/3 taxable earnings and 2/3 after tax dollars she invested. She can allow her remaining $75,000 to continue to grow for later use. With the help of a trusted financial advisor, she would be able to take advantage of this income for life.

Preparing for tax hikes is yet another way we protect you from tax issues. The debt problem our country faces is likely to require an increase in taxes, even though neither Democrats nor Republicans are going to agree to call it this.

How can the government raise taxes without calling it this? In the same way they raise the debt ceiling without calling it a raise. For taxes, they will either eliminate deductions or phase out deductions, typically for the "wealthy" taxpayers.

In the coming years, those making $200,000 or more a year will have problems deducting personal exemptions for things like state taxes, charitable contributions, and even their dependents. If you earn enough money, the value of your 1040 deductions will soon go to zero. Sure, your "tax rate" did not increase, but suddenly you are paying more taxes. This has the effect of virtually raising your tax rate by 1 to two percent. After all of the deductions are phased out, once could expect the statutory top tax rate to be closer to 41%, above the 39.6% it currently is.

Can we stop these changes? Outside of campaigning to get our politicians to extend the Bush tax rates, we cannot. Our goal is to make sure that you are forewarned of these changes and how they will affect you. Awareness of this change is power, and we will make sure you are aware, and thus, empowered.

Protecting Your Long-Term Care Expenses

Along with inflation, the looming specter of long term care expenses is one of the most dangerous threats to your long-term financial well-being. When most people think of wealth management and protection, they think of retirement savings and investments. This is a valuable part of the strategy, yet we believe it is just one part of a much larger and more significant whole. Other strategies, like life insurance, long term care insurance, and estate planning are just as important.

Long Term Care Insurance

Did you know that many people have stopped buying private, long-term care coverage? In fact, Hartford and Hancock, two of the largest providers, are no longer writing these policies. What has happened to cause this change?

Historically, two things occurred to point to this change. First, people on a whole are living longer, and thus using up their benefits. Second, the pricing for the benefits did not keep up with the increasing expenditures.

For the average consumer, the costs of long-term care coverage became hard to justify. The policies were complicated and unclear, and the limitations severe. Policies require you to fund your long-term care yourself for a short period, typically between 90 and 100 days. Policyholders also face a non-inflation adjusted dollar amount. The time period and monthly limits for most policies, usually up to five years at $6,000 to $7,000 per month, is no longer realistic as people live longer and expenses increase. In today's world, people could need this care much longer than five years and spend as much as $200,000 per year for their needs.

Yet, failing to plan for your long-term care because the policies no longer make sense is not the right answer either. The good news is that the Pension Protection Act of 2006 provides the opportunity to purchase long-term care riders. Some of these will increase your income by 50 to 100% for the rest of your life should you need them. Others offer the opportunity to access hundreds of thousands, if not millions, of dollars, at any point in time, if you're eligible, at no additional risk. You deserve to see how these changes can benefit you and your long-term care needs.

Benefits of Life Insurance for the Living

In our profession, we often see couples who are not on the same page about life insurance. The man may think "The only reason they want me to get life insurance is to use my money to fund an extravagant lifestyle after I die." The wife, on the other hand, may suppose, "I have worked hard all of these years, and I deserve to be taken care of if my husband dies before me!"

These scenarios show that there are many misconceptions out there about what life insurance really is and what it can do for individuals, couples and businesses to accomplish lifetime goals. A well thought out and expertly implemented life insurance-based strategy can serve as a valuable asset. It can help provide the significant funds you need in retirement, finance a home or car purchase, or even fund a new business.

All of these important goals can easily be met with life insurance, so it can be much more than simply leaving something behind for your loved ones when you pass on. This option allows you an unmatched potential to defer taxes, or never pay them altogether, depending on how the accounts are structured. This is truly "living life insurance," and this is something the team of fiduciaries is able to help you attain.

The Private Capital Reserve Strategy:

How to the Wealth Builders Do It

Would you rather be a customer of the bank, or have and use funds more like a bank? We would rather be like the bank, because most of know that customers of the banks pay dearly.

Banks use something called the "velocity of money multiplier". After Basel III, most banks can lend up to $7-9 for every one dollar in reserves. (The discussion regarding how this happens gets real complicated, is beyond the scope of this book, and is best left to other resources. To understand completely how this works, begin by asking how central banks "create" money). We, unfortunately, cannot get that kind of multiplier. What if we could get 1.5-2X multipliers? We can. Here is how.

We begin by first understanding how we pay for everything, how compounding really works, and the differences between being a debtor, saver, and wealth creator. We finance everything we buy.

This bears repeating. We finance every-thing we buy. We either use other people's money and pay them interest. Or, we use our own money, and give up interest and earnings. Let that sink in a moment.

Therefore, many of us arbitrage. This only means that we weigh how much the banks charge us versus how much we could be earning. Or we have a misconception about how money works. Even our own money is only "rented". We cannot take it with us. So we try to be good stewards of our money for as long we can have access, use, and control over it.

And if you have no access to the capital (as in your government qualified retirement account prior to age 59.5; or in your house equity, unless you sell it, or buy a mortgage -- if you qualify), and you have no ability to use and control your money (how much control do you have over your investments, or your house value?), is it truly yours?

Next let's explore how some use money. Debtors begin with nothing, and borrow against future earnings to pay back the debt. Savers build up their capital, then spend it down, only to have to rebuild for use later. Wealth creators, figure out how keep their own money, continue to earn a safe return, and still use other people's money to finance purchases.

Regarding debt, we believe you should not be a debtor. Yet you have heard that if you borrow $1 million, the bank owns you; if you borrow $1 billion, you own the bank; and if you borrow $1 trillion, you are the banking system. Are you truly a debtor if you have $1million earning a safe return, with immediate access, use, and control and simultaneously owe $1 million? Of course not. You are net even.

We believe you should have all your assets paid for. That is the safe way. That is how savers do it. What if there were a safer way? There can be a better way to have an asset paid for than merely not owing. We believe it is having the $1 million asset and having the $1 million in a safe, easily accessible, compounding, account, while owing the same $1 million to a lending institution. (At this point, it is beyond the scope of this book, and not very meaningful to discuss the rate of interest owed versus the rate of return you could earn, i.e. "arbitrage".) This is the wealth creator way.

We now must engage in more discussion about compounding. When does all the benefit achieve meaning? Over time. In fact, over time, the compounding can be astounding with enormous results.

Example: we paid for Manhattan island about 400 years ago with $24 in Wampum, remember? We know that real estate returns 1-2% over inflation over very long periods of time. (Yes, some people get higher rates of return, but only through, work such as development, speculation, or through leveraging the property). We also know that inflation has averaged 3.5% over that same period of time. The last time we checked, the entire value of all real estate in all of New York's five boroughs -- not just Manhattan -- was about $680 billion. We also know that if you compound $24 at 5.5% daily, the net amount is about $1.1 trillion. We are pretty close. Is compounding not wonderful?

It is, especially if it goes un-delayed, un-interrupted, and un-taxed. Delaying, interrupting, or taxing drastically reduces the compounding effects. The "curve shifts way to the right". And there are several types of accounts that allow compounding to occur without taxation. Delay is up to you. Interruption can be avoided by using the Private Capital Reserve Strategy.

So imagine, you are eligible to have placed after-tax dollars in this account. You do it right away. You do this over and over again. Like any business it takes time to properly capitalize.

After a few years, there is "critical capital mass". It grows at a reasonable 3, 4, or 5% compounding rate. It is tax-deferred growth. It is tax-free growth. And it is safe. You will never lose your money. You can access this capital at any time, for any reason, completely tax-free. Now you have all this capital built up, just like a bank.

But how do you access this capital? Do you take it out? Borrow from it? No, you leave it in the account, and pledge it as collateral. You have built up sufficient "collateral capacity". And you borrow against it. Because amortizing interest never out-runs compound interest.

Amortizing interest means that you pay less interest with every payment, because more goes toward paying down principal. While your compound interest account continues to grow. As you pay back the amortizing note, your compounding effect continues to your benefit. Compounding always outruns amortization.

Thus, you keep your own money growing, while paying for the privilege of using other people's money. And you can construct the re-payments in unlimited variations.

You are in control. You can pay it back fast or slow. You can skip payments if you must, of if you want. The faster you pay it down, the greater your collateral capacity grows for the next major purchase. You can delay all payments until you are no longer on this earth. If you anticipate no major purchases...Well, you get the picture. This is how the wealth builders do it.

Life Insurance

Nick Murray, the father of Certified Financial Planners, says that insurance is the backbone of any financial plan. We may not like paying for it, but we all desire the security insurance affords.

During the discovery process, we will look at your life and finances and find areas where you have high risk. Whenever possible, we will transfer that risk from you to an insurance "carrier" or company. Insurance companies know how to price risk in a way that is acceptable to you as the policy holder while also providing them sufficient funds to make a pay out when necessary.

As you look for financial help, you will find that financial advisors often fall into two camps. One says to never buy insurance because it is too expensive. The other says never to invest in stocks or bonds because they are too risky. We believe they are each right and wrong.

Insurance and investments are just tools. No tool can be, in and of itself, wrong or right. We believe in a process, not a product. If those tools help you reach your financial goals, then they are right for you, but if not, then you should forgo them. You need a complete toolbox full of a variety of tools, not just a box packed with screwdrivers. By focusing on the process, you can choose the right insurance, when necessary, to help protect your investments. Knowing which insurance, how much, how to apply insurance can bring tremendous value to your family, your favorite charity, and to your legacy. Too many of us are under-insured.

Turning to Trusts for a Return on Life

As we shared before, insurance is the back bone of any financial plan. (Not just life insurance, of course, but too many of us are inappropriately insured, with regards to life insurance in particular). Let us examine how life insurance can help your future financial goals. Irrevocable life insurance trusts, or ILITs, can preserve an inheritance and reduce estate tax burdens for beneficiaries. Life insurance is a critical component of a solid financial and tax planning strategy. The first reason most people buy life insurance is to safeguard families in the event of a breadwinner's death, helping to ensure that daily living expenses are met, college tuitions are paid, and children can remain in the home they grew up in, nevertheless this is just the primary reason. Another reason to buy life insurance, whole life in particular, is to create an emergency fund that can be borrowed against, tax-free, should it be needed.

Whole life insurance has a cash value that increases with time, provided the premiums are consistently paid. These are very reliable accounts. In fact, there has only been one company in the UK, Canada, and the United States over the last 200 years that failed to meet its obligation, and that was Executive Life in New York in the 1980s. Even in this scenario, the policyholders received 98 cents on the dollar.

Why do whole life insurance providers do so well? First, they generate fees, so even if a company goes under, the next company will buy them for the ongoing fees. This makes them an attractive option, and thus they rarely go completely under without being bought out by someone else. Also, each company is required to have reinsurance in case something bad happened. Funds are kept in separate accounts and not co-mingled with the insurance carrier's investment funds. Finally, many states have a program similar to the FDIC that provides protection for these life insurance funds.

So, regardless of whether markets go up or down, the cash value continues to grow on whole life insurance policies. Your death benefit, therefore, remains intact and growing. Not only can life insurance fund your long-term needs, but it also is a highly effective tool to provide tax-free income to heirs and help ensure that estate taxes owed can be paid. This is particularly important now that estate tax uncertainties may linger for a few years.

When you are planning your life insurance policy, you will want to take advantage of the various trusts that are out there that provide a tax shelter. Before choosing an option, however, you will need the help of a financial advisor. Some trusts, like the irrevocable life insurance trust, do not give he grantor access to the cash. Others provide excellent asset protection and estate planning with fewer restrictions and the power to borrow against the policy. Careful, life insurance is complicated, and there is a possible mis-alignment of interests regarding life insurance and their commissions. A fee-based advisor can help provide you with the proper information to make great decisions about life insurance.

Protecting Your Long-Term Wealth

Wealth management and protection is not a one-step process. We are firm believers in our process, rather than products, and that process has four basic steps. Those steps all point towards one goal – to guarantee you income for life.

First, we need to focus on your immediate income. It does no good to save for retirement if you cannot put food on the table now. While your income is comfortable at the moment, you need to be certain that you can survive if something unexpected, like a serious business downturn or loss of a job, occurs. This is why the first step is to put enough money in a money market account or similar short-term savings venue to give you two years of income with an additional six months of emergency money. If you do not need to tap into this, it will fund the first two years of your retirement.

Once that is ready, we are going to start setting money into an account that will pay out over eight years. With the investment and returns on this account, it will be sufficient to cover your expenses for eight years, even if you earn nothing during this time. For the first 10 years of your retirement, you have guaranteed income. At the end of 10 years, these two legs are exhausted.

However, during these 10 years, the third part of the plan has a chance to grow. Here are your investments and your stock portfolio. All of the returns they have earned are part of step three. If handled properly, this should give you enough money to live out the remainder of your life.

Step four is your reserves. This is the money that you have set aside for emergencies, to cover inflation, to fund healthcare expenses, etc. Whatever extra you have, it goes to step four to be used for these purposes.

In each of these steps, you have a range of products you can use to invest your money. Our job is to find the programs out of the hundreds and hundreds out there that will fit into these steps. We compare them, analyze them, and help you make great decisions with the proper information.

While there are literally hundreds of options out there, we have found that our clients tend to focus on just a few of them. Some of these are as follows:

Annuities

An ugly word for some. Many of us have an extremely negative view of annuities. And with good reason. Too many were sold, yet not bought and implemented for the right reasons, and in the right way. Yet, why do so many of us love the social security payments we receive, or wish we had a pension? These are nothing more than annuities.

Pension Annuities

Should you consider a pension annuity? To answer this question, consider 17th century Europe. Toward the end of the century, power brokers faced a problem similar to the ones facing many aging cities in the 21st century. Politicians made promises to pay lifetime pensions, but inaccurately estimated the costs of those liabilities. At the same time, insurance companies were offering annuities to people of all ages, but were charging them a flat, fixed price regardless of how old or young they were. Some historians claim that the French Treasury issued life annuities instead of regular bonds at extreme, generous yields that were the same for young and old. This led to the initial bankruptcy of the Treasury, eventually causing the French Revolution. While it looked like a good idea on paper, it did not work when put into practice.

Why is this? Well, consider this practical question. Would it make more sense for you to get a lifetime pension annuity of $1,000 per month or a lump sum of $300,000? Are you better off taking the money out of retirement savings to buy your own annuity? These are vital questions, and for many retirees, they could be the most important financial questions they ask.

Let us take a closer look at them. If you could have $3,000 a month starting at age 70 for the rest of your life, or $306,000 in a lump sum payment, which one would you take? The $3,000 a month adds up to $36,000 a year. That must be multiplied by 8.5 to equal $306,000. That is similar to an interest rate of between seven and eight percent. What does this mean? It means the only reason to take the lump sum payment is if interest rates are above 7.5%. If they are six percent, you are better off taking the annuity than the larger lump sum.

The famous astronomer, Edmond Halley of Halley Comet's fame, was asked to look at this problem with pension annuities, and he posted an article on it in 1693. In the article, he proposed the formula used in the scenario we just discussed. Your numbers probably do not exactly match the scenario, but we can use that calculation to determine if a pension annuity makes sense for your unique set of financial circumstances. It may or it may not, but you cannot make this decision without the right information.

Annuities provide a continuous stream of income. It is that simple. Money Magazine recently addressed this question: What portion of my 401(k) and savings should I move to annuities? The answer was excellent, "that depends." You see, annuities have fees, and those fees are sometimes quite high. Some describe these fees in emotional terms as "onerous" or "excessive." Others will go so far as to say that annuities are overall a bad investment option. Yet, annuities are nothing more than an insurance product geared to consume an estate while providing the protection that you will never run out of money.

Would you view car insurance as "bad" or "unnecessary?" What about your homeowner's insurance? Is that too expensive? Probably, you would answer "no." We feel the same way. We believe that insurance is not bad; it is simply a tool. There cannot be a bad tool. There can, however, be a bad use of a tool.

Here is what we believe are the three great attributes of annuities:

1. They guarantee your principal
2. They guarantee a rate of return
3. They guarantee your income

These are excellent guarantees, and we all know how few places offer a true guarantee these days. Outside of government pensions, which in theory are guaranteed, annuities through insurance companies are one of the only ways to guarantee future income. This means they can be a valuable part of your comprehensive financial plan as you seek to augment your income needs.

However, annuities have a bad side too. They are not meant to be an investment, so do not buy one if you do not need these guarantees. Annuities are not liquid to the point where you can get all of your money out. You can however take 10% of your investment completely penalty-free, but that is all.

Yes, there are fees and costs associated with annuities. Although, when you realize it is an insurance product, this makes sense. You pay for your other insurance products, so you will pay for this one as well. As we commonly say, "there is no free lunch." As you can see, the answer to whether one should own an annuity is "it depends." This insurance may be right for you, or it may be completely wrong. Only through trusted advice can you make this decision for yourself.

If you do think that annuities may be a good idea, remember that there are different types that provide different guarantees. Also, some annuities do carry risk. Ask a trusted Summit advisor to assist in exploring this option – we can help.

Variable Annuities

Variable annuities are a type of hybrid, part stock market exposure and part insurance product of a traditional annuity. The purpose of an annuity is to guarantee income. The purpose of the markets is trying to achieve growth. When put together, they are like oil and vinegar. In the right proportion, on the proper salad, they work fantastic, but when paired disproportionately, they may not work as well as expected. In fact, we've seen variable annuities with expenses exceeding 6, 7, 8, 9 and even 11% on occasion. This is not typical; these annuities typically have around a three percent expense ratio.

Now, suppose you are a relatively conservative investor and you've got 80% of your variable annuity in the bond market, and the bond market's returning two percent. Well, not only are you losing one percent because of the three percent expense ratio, but you are also losing another two, three and four percent depending on the inflation rate. Not a good combination. These plans can work, but you have to have the right information to make the right choices, and often the insurance providers are not willing or able to provide enough information.

In fact, many variable annuity carriers are hunkering down, and despite demand on the part of advisors, these insurers are steering clear of additional exposure. Some have completely exited the variable annuity markets. So ask yourself this question: if the insurers are not willing to take on the risk of the markets, as well as the risk of guaranteeing that they will pay you, why should you take on the same risk? If you are going to pay an insurance company to transfer the risk of longevity and obtain lifelong guaranteed income, why would you then take back that risk and expose yourself to the markets? This is what variable annuities, in effect, do.

LLC Structures

This is not the place to talk in detail about asset protection and wealth preservation strategies. For that, reference a book I coauthored called, "Cover Your Assets." Here we will give a glimpse of what could be done. *www.mysummitwealth.com/media-publications.*

An LLC can be an asset protection device because of a charging order. This gives the creditor the right to any distributions that the LLC makes to its members. If there are no distributions, there is nothing for the creditor to take. If there is a profit, a tax is owed, even if no distributions are made. The creditor getting the charging order would have to pay this tax, even without getting paid.

The way you structure your LLC can actually play a role in how well your assets are protected. Take a look at a Florida Supreme Court case to understand why.

On June 24, 2010, the Florida Supreme Court issues a long-awaited decision in a closely watched case. In the Olmstead Decisions, the defendant was a single member limited liability company, or LLC. Because he was a single member LLC, Olmstead received no protection through the charging order. The state legislature provides this protection only to multi member LLCs. Single member LLCs, like Olmstead, were not offered this protection. In fact, they have no asset protection mechanisms whatsoever.

Many individuals are not aware of this, and we believe this is a problem. In order to have the asset protection of an LLC, you have to bring on another member, and we strongly recommend that you restructure your estate in this way to gain this protection.

Now, this member does not have to be another individual or someone outside of your family or estate. You can set up your children's irrevocable trust to be a member, or you could have your spouse come in as a managing member. You stay the managing member, and thus have control over how the LLC is managed.

You can still access any cash value of your LLC, and anything left when you die would simply transfer to the other member, such as your children's trust. By doing this, you ensure that you continue to receive asset protection through your LLC structure. Ask us to determine if and how an LLC can protect your estate – we can help.

These are just a few of the ways we work to protect your long-term wealth and income. We will discuss actual investment strategies in the next chapter, with a discussion of estate planning later as well.

Key Takeaways
- Avoiding the losses is more powerful than picking the winners
- First protect, *then* optimize
- Seek to be a Wealth Builder
- Compounding always outruns amortization
- Life insurance is the spine of all financial plans

Chapter 4: How to Deal with Fear Mongers and Portfolio Killers

"We love to expect, and when expectation is either disappointed or gratified, we want to be again expecting."

–Samuel Johnson

Expectations and Investment Decisions:

Having the knowledge to make informed decisions

One of the most important duties is providing you with the information to have realistic expectations about the performance of your investments and the fulfillment of your plan. The right expectations should be the primary focus driving investment decisions, not emotions, costs, or even past performance. The correct expectations allow for an evidenced-based, logical approach to investing and wealth management. You must also be able to distinguish between gambling and speculation versus prudent investing. We believe that is the best way to approach planning for, and taking control of the future -- a confident future.

Looking at the Lost Decade

The years 1999 to 2000 are often called the "Lost Decade" by investment and finance writers. During these years, the S&P 500 index was completely dominated by large growth stocks. These stocks had done so well that many investors were invested almost completely in this one index. Those who committed 100% of their money to the S&P 500 at the beginning of the decade lost significantly, because by the end of 2009, annualized pre-tax returns on the S&P 500 were −1.1%. But, was it really a lost decade? Honestly, we do not think so. Take a look at the following chart

Not **Everyone** Lost During "The Lost Decade"

Year	Conservative	Moderate	Growth	Aggressive
	$100,000	$100,000	$100,000	$100,000
2000	5.3%	3.0%	0.7%	- 1.7%
2001	5.3%	2.9%	0.4%	- 2.3%
2002	1.00/	7 70/	0 50/	17 70/
2003	**5.43**	**6.11**	**6.31**	**6.07**
2004				
2005	4.1%	7.21%	10.3%	13.1%
2006	9.0%	13.9%	18.5%	22.4%
2007	4.0%	3.6%	3.1%	3.1%
2008	- 5.5%	- 17.5%	- 29.9%	- 39.1%
2009	10.5%	19.6%	28.7%	36.1%
Return	$169,637	$180,916	$184,476	$180,232

As you can see, some people had the ability to do quite well during this decade, with annualized returns of over nine percent in some cases. Even the laziest buy and hold investor could have bought a mix of "garden variety," passively managed funds, not rebalanced the portfolio, not added a dime to it, and still achieved quite satisfactory returns. The catch? They had to be invested in more than just US growth stocks.

In fact, investors should have known this. In 1999, the idea of growth stocks' susceptibility to bubbles, and the long-term, observed premium of value stocks, was hardly new. The information was freely available with a simple look at history, so committing 100% of your money in December 1999 to the S&P 500 would simply be a poor choice, especially with the readily available alternatives.

Remember, the S&P 500 is not *the* stock market, but rather one component of many. It represents only U.S. Large companies. Do not limit yourself by focusing entirely on one index.

Simple diversification has worked well over the past decade. In fact, it has worked well for eons, and it will continue to prove to be the most reliable and strategically successful method of investing. Knowledge regarding how markets work creates appropriate expectations. If your knowledge of markets is uncertain, you may be disappointed as results do not meet expectations

So, what does this have to do with your expectations? The moral of this story is this: no one can know in advance which asset class will perform well. Trying to beat or time the markets is a gamble. Those who claim they can tell you to expect a certain return are wrong and doomed to failure. If you follow them, you place your money at risk. However, there is a solution.

If you are serious about your money and want long-term success that reaps good returns reliably, consistently, and predictably, then you want Prudent Investing, not gambling and speculating. The three signs of gambling and speculating are:

1. Stock Picking
2. Market Timing
3. Track Record Chasing.

Gambling and Speculating

Investing and gambling have much in common, especially when your focus is to beat the markets. When you gamble, emotions are high, and you often make decisions for purely emotional reasons. The same thing occurs when you invest, and it leads to big mistakes.

Consider, for example, the "dot.coms" at the turn of the year 2000. People told themselves, "I'm investing in e-commerce," when in fact they were not at all. They were buying shares in companies that made no money. The companies raised equity with the sole intention of burning through it, as they attempted to build clicks or gather unique visitors. They were not, actually, selling anything.

Also, "e-commerce" as a business model had never made any money. After all, the model and infrastructure had not existed five years earlier. This meant that the expectations of those who were investing in the dot.coms had no foundation or assurance. There was no justification for the risk.

Putting money into an enterprise that has no assurance of success or previous track record of income is not investing. It is speculating or gambling.

What does this mean for you? You need to have the ability to distinguish between investment and speculation, because the difference is the foundation for your expectations for a particular investment option. Remember, all short-term trading is speculation, because fundamental values do not change quickly. An investor is always looking for long-term growth.

Similarly, all options and all futures contracts are speculation, because their ending value after expiration is zero. Therefore, buying an option or futures contract is speculation on a change in the price of the underlying security or commodity, as opposed to an investment in the security's fundamental value.

Distinguishing between investments and speculation can be challenging. For example, Microsoft's common stocks would be considered an investment. However, the September 30 Microsoft call, is speculation. Gold is an investment, albeit a poor one if standing alone, but a futures contract for the delivery of gold in November, is speculation. Hedge funds are always speculation, because the creator of the hedge has no interest in the fundamental value of the securities or commodities he's hedging. He just wants the spread to increase or decrease so he can make money.

Now, if hedges, futures contracts and options are speculation, not investing, what are professionally managed portfolios that have these instruments but are diversified? Are they investments? Should you even include such managers in your portfolio?

These are good questions, and ones you must answer before you can have a realistic expectation for your potential future income. You need to completely understand the basic risks, rewards and strategies of these funds, so you can avoid making emotional decisions. This is where we can help.

Stock Picking

Stock picking is getting trickier, so you need to get picky about picking stocks. In fact, we would caution you against stock picking altogether.

A year ago, stocks were moving in such unison that traditional fund managers couldn't hope to beat the market. The average large cap fund has returned just 4.5% in 2011, according to Morningstar, compared with the S&P 500 index, which is up about five percent.

Average U.S. Equity Mutual Fund
36 Year Period

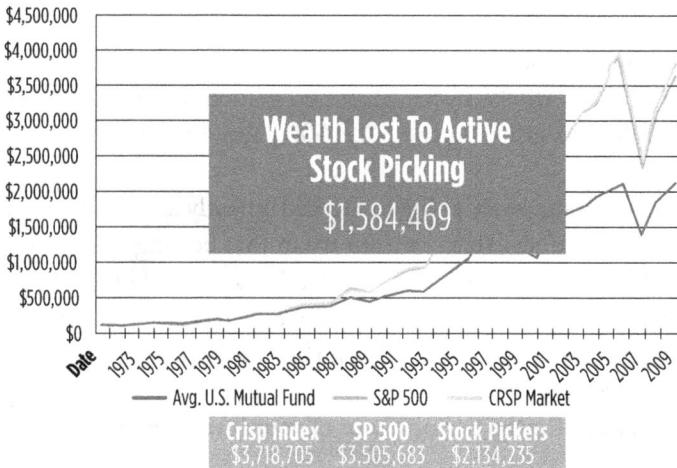

Legend: Avg. U.S. Mutual Fund — S&P 500 — CRSP Market

Crisp Index	SP 500	Stock Pickers
$3,718,705	$3,505,683	$2,134,235

Wealth Lost To Active Stock Picking $1,584,469

Only 31% of stock pickers outperformed relative benchmarks in the first six months of 2011. This is compared to the historical six-month average of 41%. According to the Wall Street Journal, that means that historically, only about two out of five stock pickers who run the best mutual funds and hedge funds in the world are able to beat the markets.

And yet, in the first two months of 2011, less than one out of three were able to beat the markets. Is there any rhyme or reason to this? Which ones are going to succeed? Which sectors? Which industries? Anyone who pretends to know this is not being realistic.

Some managers will try to assure you that you will succeed at stock picking if you pick within certain industries. Before you believe this, here are a few statistics from 2011 to keep in mind:

- A full 64% of financial services under performed the S&P 500
- Around 75% of consumer staples and healthcare stocks beat the S&P 500
- Only 43% of tech stocks outperformed

What about size? Does size matter? Can you form your expectations about stock performance, thus picking the winners, based on the size of the stock? Consider these statistics:

- The 50 biggest stocks in the S&P 500 gained just 2.9%
- The 50 smallest stocks in the S&P 500 gained 4.5%
- The middle 100 stocks in the S&P 500 gained 9.1%

Predicting which stocks are going to succeed is nearly impossible and relies significantly on chance. That does not mean that beating the market isn't possible. What is impossible is to do so reliably, consistently and predictably. For this reason, as we have emphasized, we focus on diversifying rather than trying to pick the winning stocks. This will bring reliable, consistent and predictable results more than stock picking ever could, giving you solid expectations for the performance of your investments.

Expectations Tainted by Anxiety

The affluent are feeling anxious about their financial expectations. Recent research clearly shows this:

- 66% are concerned about rising healthcare costs
- 58% worry their money will run out in retirement
- 52% worry about the economy's impact on the ability to meet financial goals (taxes and inflation)
- 39% are worried about supporting lifestyle

The rest worry about the direction of our country and civilization

This shows that people need a consistent and expert financial voice, a private wealth advocate, if you will, in order to empower full financial health.

If you are facing similar anxieties, you probably do not have your proper protections and guarantees in place. You have good reason to be anxious, because you may not be prepared for the next "great big financial storm."

The difference between us and other advisors is that we recognize the three types of money: lifestyle, accumulated, and wealth transfer money. Everyone recognizes the lifestyle and accumulated money, and "gurus" like Dave Ramsey or Suzie Orman will tell you the only solution to increasing your accumulated money is to cut your lifestyle, yet who really wants to do that? Others, like Jim Cramer, will tell you that you need to take that accumulated money and try to earn a little bit more, but as we have shown, those extra potential returns require more risk. Who wants to do that?

Should "Sunk" Cost Impact Investment Decisions?

The price paid for investments often becomes an emotional hang up for people. This is natural, but it can be fatal to your investment goals. Your cost in an investment has nothing to do with its objective value today. After all, the investments do not know nor do they care what you paid for them. They are going to behave the way they behave regardless of how much they cost. As soon as you buy an investment, your cost is set, and it will either perform or it will not perform.

A focus on the cost of investments can lead to two common investment mistakes. The first is refusing to diversify after succeeding because of the capital gains taxes you would pay to sell. At current rates, paying 15% in taxes to realize a great gain is a rare opportunity, and if you have it you should consider jumping on it. This would give you the chance to redeploy your money with lower risks to earn consistent and predictable returns. Yet, many people fail to sell because they cannot see past the number of dollars in taxes they would have to pay to do so. This ignores the greater benefit and the greater risk, and actually encourages you to behavior more risky, and this is a cost you should try to avoid.

A second big mistake is taking the attitude of "I can't afford the loss." If you have an investment that has dropped in value, you cannot afford not to take the loss. The price now is what the investment is worth now. The price also reflects all known and knowable information. It might be worth more in the future, or it might be worth even less. If it is time to sell and redistribute your money, do not let a loss keep you from doing so.

By working with a fee-based financial advisor, who puts your interests ahead of her own, and benefiting from trusted advice, you can remove your emotions from the money and get the information you need to make great decisions.

The Truth of Fees and Costs in Investing

Investing involves fees and costs, and expenses. This is something we, as investors, accept. However, disclosures of these expenses are often difficult for clients to interpret. They are imbedded into legalese and buried in a tiny font at the bottom of the page of your investment agreement. We believe clients want and deserve a clear understanding of these fees and costs so they can invest wisely and confidently. We also believe they should know what many others are paying with other advisors.

Truth about fees and costs can be a bit disturbing. For example, it may upset you to discover that you could be paying more than six percent in taxes and fess unknowingly and unnecessarily on your investments each year. This is sadly the case when compounding occurs before inflation and before paying advisory fees.

Have you ever taken the time to read a mutual fund or exchange traded fund's prospectus? This document discloses the Net Expense Ratio, or NER, yet few people take the time to read it. Why? Because of the legalese it contains and the small font that makes it difficult, if not impossible, to read. Without reading this document, you may not realize just how much that fund is costing you.

According to Morningstar, the average NER for a stock mutual fund has risen subtly and steadily from 1.39% in 1987 to over 1.52% by October 2010. That number may continue to rise toward two percent. Higher still are "small cap" funds with an NER of 1.61%, and international funds with an NER of 1.68%.

While some of us may take the time to read the NER, even fewer of us read the Statement of Additional Information (SAI), which describes the activities and additional fund expenses, costs and fees on the fund. One of the most misunderstood or understated of these is the trading activity in the fund.

Morningstar shows that the average mutual fund has a stock turnover of about 115% per year nearly every year. How is that for activity? That means if there are 100 stocks in a particular fund at the beginning of the year, by the end of the year at least 100 of those same stocks have been sold, with a handful of others also having been bought and then sold during this time. Often, investors end up several of the same stocks in the overall portfolio. We consider this incredibly inefficient.

Roger Edelen of Boston College, Richard Evans of the University of Virginia, and Gregory Kedlec of Virginia Polytechnical Institute discussed this in an article titled "Scale Affects in Mutual Performance" in a 2007 issue of Registered Representative Magazine. In the article the researchers found that the SAI reports had an additional trading cost, on average, of 1.44% per year. According to the Zero Alpha Group on FundPolice.com, they found that the average fund annual expense ratio was 1.72%.

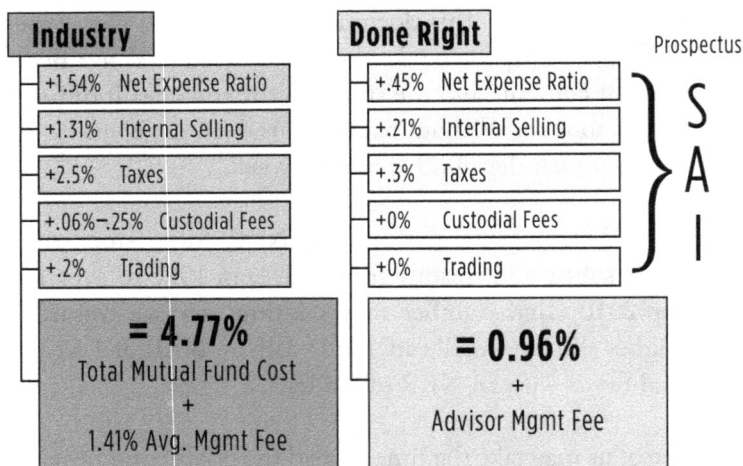

Industry		**Done Right**		Prospectus
+1.54%	Net Expense Ratio	+.45%	Net Expense Ratio	
+1.31%	Internal Selling	+.21%	Internal Selling	S
+2.5%	Taxes	+.3%	Taxes	A
+.06%–.25%	Custodial Fees	+0%	Custodial Fees	I
+.2%	Trading	+0%	Trading	

= 4.77%
Total Mutual Fund Cost
+
1.41% Avg. Mgmt Fee

= 0.96%
+
Advisor Mgmt Fee

Each of these trading activities cause a taxable event, which causes investors to lose, on average, an additional 2.5% of their returns to taxes, as revealed on the SEC website in 2006. Overlooking this expense is too easy.

To determine the true cost of a simple mutual fund, all of these fees must be combined, and Ray J. Shreder, RFC, CRC, AIF states that, when all of the data is taken together, the industry average is as high as 4.01 to 5.46% annually!

Unfortunately, that's not all. On top of those expenses, the average financial advisor charges 1.41%, according to Tiburon's Strategic Advisors, the fee-only financial advisors' Best Practices Survey. Allan Ross of CBS's MoneyWatch.com reported on August 17, 2009 that mutual fund fees had jumped a full five percent. Because of all of these somewhat hidden costs, Morningstar admits on the "My Money Blog" that fund expenses should be more important than star ratings when choosing a financial advisor.

Keep in mind that you will pay custodial fees of 0.06 to .25% for Schwab, TD Ameritrade, Fidelity or Wells Fargo to hold your assets. And there are costs associated with trading the funds themselves, which can be around 0.2%.

Do you feel overwhelmed yet? Our research clearly shows that, using outside funds, total costs to you can exceed 4.77%, so your fund must earn at least five percent for you to break even! And we all know how challenging that five percent figure can be in a down economy.

We believe that there is a better, more affordable solution, that our clients should not be paying nearly five percent in fees and taxes to invest their money.

So what is the solution to this problem?

First, if you are not investing for the long term, you probably do not need the risk. Yet who of us really is not a long-term investor. Considering the average 60 year old couple has a 30 year retirement, most of us can be categorized "long-term." Those who leave a legacy by definition are planning for the long haul. Saving for college in the next 10 years is not, considering that there have been 20 year periods when investing has been "flat." Likewise, there have been 30 year periods when bonds (loans) outperformed stocks (ownership). So to make the point more clear, be certain not to confuse savings and investments. Any time you may need to access the capital, not the earnings, in less than 10 years, there probably ought to be a savings plan, not an investment plan.

The word investing brings fear to the minds of the uninformed person looking for a way to secure their future. We all know that investing brings risk, and the ultimate goal is monetary reward. Understanding the balance between that risk and reward is where many people fail. At Summit Wealth, our goal is to help you find the right balance to meet your needs through informed discovery. With the right information, you can make great decisions.

Euphoria, Fear, and Panic

Having the right expectations about market performance can help ward off another investment mistake we see, and that is allowing fear to drive your decisions. Sometimes this manifests as euphoria, or the complete loss of a true sense of danger. When euphoria hits you, you no longer fear principal loss, and you may refuse to accept the possibility of danger of this happening.

When this happens, your only concern becomes that some other investor, somewhere else owns funds or stocks that are going to beat yours.

Consider this example. In 1999, an investor who realized a 29% return in a properly risk-managed and diversified, high quality investment portfolio, is reported to have sued his investment advisor. Why? The investor's peers, with whom he played golf, boasted returns in excess of 70%.

In early 2000 as the market imploded, the lawsuit evaporated, but this story still shows what euphoria can do. You might ask yourself this: how would you have felt and reacted to learn that your portfolio "under-performed?" Would you have reacted the same way?

Remember, all new booms end in busts. It is difficult to know we are in a bubble until it bursts. Remember, this time is no different. The law of unintended consequences will always persist. So stand your ground on your well-managed, diversified portfolio. In euphoric times, be willing to look foolish. When the bubble bursts, you will look rich.

Euphoria is just one way in which fear, rather than knowledge, can impact your investment decisions. Panic is the other. It has been said, "you can manage tomorrow's panic by managing today's euphoria." By making wise, evidence-based, and well guided decisions when you are tempted to give in to euphoria, you will not be tipped into panic when the bubble bursts.

If you were to talk to an experienced investor, someone who has invested over decades through big ugly bear markets, you would hear the philosophy that the biggest bear markets follow and simply correct the biggest bull markets. For example, 1915 through 1928 was followed by 1929 to 1952. More recently, 2003 through 2007 was followed by 2008 to 2009.

Remember, not everything is as it seems, and it is not as good as we might hope. Thankfully, it is also rarely as bad as we feel. There is an inverse and close relationship between the height of the euphoria at the top of a big bull market and the depth of their panic-induced capitulation at the bottom of a bear.

Having this realistic understanding of the markets will keep you from sinking into despair when the lows hit. You can protect yourself from panic by proper asset allocation. If you are invested for the long term, over 20 years, then you might consider allocating very little to stocks. There has never been a 20 year period of time when stock investors have lost money had they stayed invested and diversified properly, especially after re-investing dividends. But, it could happen, so you need to allocate appropriately, preparing yourself to catch the upside when it occurs and being ready to roll with the gut punch when it comes as well.

Remember, the financial world is not going to end; it only appears to be ending. All things must pass, according to the Beatles' George Harrison. It follows that all market declines are temporary, because the market is simply a reflection of the human condition and its proxy, the economy. We humans, as a species, are continuously better off. We are better off than 20, 50, 100, or 1000 years ago. Western society and values continue to grow and with it, our human condition will continue on its upward trajectory. That is why the markets rise – inexorably and permanently.

This is the genius of the free-market capitalism system, which is the most universal and powerful force in the world. Remember, not only is this time not different, but also "this time" is never different and it never will be different. Panic is the counter-factual, irrational loss of faith in our culture, our species and the future. You cannot destroy ambition and opportunity and progress, because these are hard-wired in our genetic code.

The Media's Impact on Investment Expectations

One thing that impacts most investor's expectations for their investments is the media. When we see stories of people or firms beating the markets on the local media, we often believe that this is what our own investments should be doing. Unfortunately, the "beat the markets" claim is often nothing more than smoke and mirrors.

For example the S&P 500 averaged an annual return of approximately 5.5% over the past 50 years. But simply adding back dividends, which have averaged 3.5% over that same period of time, brings the average annual return o the S&P 500 to nine percent. Now, understand that when you buy an index fund, the dividends are typically reinvested into the fund. In other words, these companies claiming in the media to "beat the markets" are not counting dividends when measuring market performance. Yet, when they measure their own funds, they do include dividends. So, they are not comparing apples to apples. This is just one way that the media and large firms taint your expectations.

The Securities and Exchange Commission requires mutual funds to include dividend income in the performance of the index they are measuring against. Money managers abiding by voluntary guidelines known as the Global Investment Performance Standards, or GIPS, must do the same. Financial advisors and newsletter publishers, among other "pros," are not always covered by such rules.

One website shows cumulative gain of the S&P 500 since January 2005 at 12.5%. Naturally, that number fails to include dividends. When dividends are included, the actual annual rate of growth soars to 28.1%. The portfolio manager in question boasts a 15% annual return over that time period, claiming that he beat the index by three percent. When you factor in dividends, however, he actually under performed by about 50%.

Jim Cramer once sent out an email that said, "My portfolio is CRUSHING the S&P 500." The email goes on to say that the portfolio's "total average return has averaged more than DOUBLE the return of the S&P 500." And there is an accompanying bar graph that showed that the S&P 500 returned 15.5% versus 39.2% for Mr. Cramer's portfolio. Once again, when you add in dividends, the S&P 500 returned 38.3%. This is a far cry from "CRUSHING" the S&P 500. In fact, the returns are nearly identical.

Had you bought and held an S&P 500 index fund, and then done literally nothing with it except reinvest your dividends, you too would have "doubled the market," as long as you did not factor in the dividends when making the calculation. So, the next time you hear a portfolio manager boasting about consistently beating the markets, take it with a grain of salt. The sad truth is that many so-called professionals will say anything at all to attract investors. They are not looking out for your best interests.

Beware of Financial Entertainers

Financial entertainers, which are the faces you see on the TV all the time, have been jumping up and down crying about how we are facing the end of the world as we know it. This can send many investors into a panic, yet this is just an example of the "Disaster du Jour."

Remember 1991 and 1992, just after the savings and loan crisis and just before that powerful nine-year bull market? During those years, you heard much of the same claims. They just did not seem as loud since we did not have the Internet. With the World Wide Web, it is much easier for the "noise makers" to get our attention.

The one reason that these media "gurus" give for feeling that the bear market has a long way to go before it is going to improve is the current excessive debt situation. Debt "doomers" come in a variety of styles, according to Ken Fisher. Some point to debt as the foundation for a banking crisis, while others point to the real estate implosion. Sometimes they are linked, with claims that "falling real estate prices will bankrupt the banks which will cause chaos." Some also point to the tapped out consumer, who can't or won't borrow, who is causing the anemic recovery. These talking heads say they expect this to continue until finally we enter a double dip recession. In their minds, this is inevitable.

The Income Pyramid

To whom are they selling?

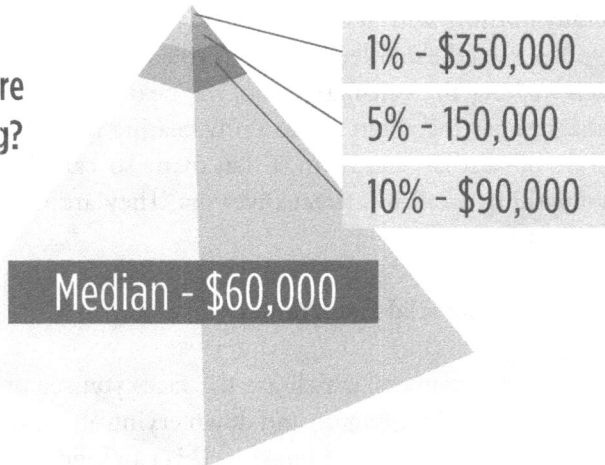

1% - $350,000

5% - 150,000

10% - $90,000

Median - $60,000

Does this sound like what we are seeing today? You might be surprised to know that the information presented above was actually written in 1991 by Ken Fisher, even though it clearly applies to today's markets. Yet, the 1991 recession did not destroy the world. We recovered. People will always say that "this time is different," but we believe this to be untrue.

In fact, "this time is different" are the four most dangerous words in investing, according to the late Sir John Templeton. Instead of worrying about the "what ifs" of the future, we are ready to help you create a high quality, prudently invested financial portfolio that is diversified, properly allocated and rebalanced in a disciplined way.

The Media's Take on Market Timing

Recently we read on the front page of the Wall Street Journal's Weekend Investor this headline: "Common Sense: How to Time the Market." Here, a media giant was trying to tell you how to time your investments. While this sounds great on paper, it is something that is impossible to do.

Marketing timing is equal to gambling and speculating with your nest egg. As earlier discussed, some people use fancy terms like "tactical asset allocation" to refer to market timing, but in the end it is the same strategy. It is the desire to buy and sell assets at the precise right times to make the most out of your money. This, in theory, is a great idea, but practically it fails because no one can make these predictions accurately and consistently.

Market Timing:
"Any attempt to alter or change the mix of assets based on a prediction or forecast about the future, sometimes called "tactical asset allocation."

In the article, the writer said, "I am a working journalist, not a stockbroker or hedge fund manager. But I firmly believe anyone can manage their own investment portfolios and outperform a simple die and hold index approach."

That is fine for a journalist to say, but there is ample evidence that market timers lose money. The evidence also shows that the best fund managers who engage in market timing lose money for their clients.

Here is how market timing works, according to the article. When the market is dropping, the fund manager buys stocks at intervals of 10% declines from the most recent peak, and when it is rising, he sells at intervals of 25% gains from the most recent low. Where did these figures come from? They are basically half of the historical average losses of 20% in bear markets and gains of 50% in bull markets, a trend that has continued since 1979.

As the article went on to say, "Easy as this system sounds, and it is simple in concept, it is amazing how difficult it sometimes feels". As my kids would have said to me years ago in the 1990s, "no 'duh."

He finished the article saying that most of all, he finds investing and thinking about the markets to be both stimulating and fun. It is an adventure and a learning experience.

Now while many of us love a good adventure, we do not believe that we should have an adventure with your money. Nor should you have that adventure. We do not believe that we should use your money as a "learning experience." That is why we say, if you want stimulation and fun, go to Las Vegas. This is a great place to gamble with your money, and at least then you would realize you are gambling. Avoid falling prey to this media hype. Instead, stick with what we know will work, avoid the risks and losses, and finish with plenty of money to enjoy your current standard of living well into your future.

Key Takeaways
- Maintain realistic expectations
- Prudent investing *is not* gambling or speculating
- Stock pickers fail over the long-term
- High internal portfolio costs can kill your progress
- Remember: the financial media's job is to sell products, *not* to educate consumers

Chapter 5: Can We Keep Up with Inflation and Get Ahead?

"A good portfolio is more than a long list of good stocks and bonds. It is a balanced whole, providing the investor with protections and opportunities with respect to a wide range of contingencies."

–Harry Markowitz, Nobel Prize Laureate
Portfolio Selection: Efficient Diversification of Investments"

"

Defining Our Investment Strategy

An investment strategy is the core of any financial plan. You do have a financial plan? And the Investment Policy Statement (IPS)? We will discuss the Investment Policy Statement in particular later in this chapter.

Our view of investments may be different than what you are used to, yet remember, our goal is to help you avoid risk, rather than recover from losses. In order to understand us better, you must first understand our approach to risk and risk management.

Avoiding the losses is more powerful than picking the winners, true? If we could only have our losses back... And consistent excellence out-performs occasional brilliance. The only evidence-based, reliable, predictable, consistent, and logical strategy can be summed up in the following statement: be prudently invested, be well diversified, be properly allocated, and maintain disciplined rebalancing. This is our philosophy and our strategy. In this chapter, we will discuss these in more detail.

Being Prudently Invested

All investments carry some sort of risk. To make wise investment choices, you must first understand how you view risk, as well as how your financial advisor views it.

Risk Aversion versus Risk Seeking

In investments, risk aversions are similar to the adrenaline produced on a weekend vacation. Some people get a great rush sitting on a quiet, secluded beach. Others pursue that rush by bungee jumping from a helicopter over piranha infested waters. Investment decisions have concrete, yet very different yields depending on how much risk an individual takes. The first question anyone should ask themselves before they invest is if they are pursuing financial services to secure their future, or to assist in making a lot of money in a short period of time.

Your perception of money and the amount you need to be comfortable is going to be different than your neighbor's. This is because of the concept of "utility of money." Utility is an interesting concept, because it revolves more on your perception and necessity than the hard economic facts of supply, demand, value and cost.

For example, the utility of one million dollars will be completely different for two people because of the way they view money and the amount they feel they need to survive and be happy. A multi-millionaire may view a million dollars as a nice, but small amount, while someone in the lower middle class will view it as a windfall. Some will even view the one million dollars differently if they receive it in two segments. Others realize the superfluous nature of money much faster than those around them. Because of all of these tendencies, utility varies from one investor to the next.

Once you determine what amount of money would provide a substantial amount of utility for you, then you can start planning what you need to do to get to that point. Your timeline will also determine your risk aversion. If you need to make a lot of money in a short period of time, then you might need to be risk seeking or risk neutral. If you have the luxury of time or a smaller amount that you need, then consider being more risk averse.

The bottom line is that, while our goal is to help you avoid risk whenever possible, there are times when you need to take some risk. In finance, risk equals reward, and without some risk, you cannot see returns. Yet, taking on unnecessary risk is unwise, which is why you need a strong financial advisor on your team.

You May Have More Risk Than You Think

Most people have more risk in their portfolios than they think. As the economic climate continues to suffer, many investors have been driven to take on reckless risks with their money. We all saw the hazards of stocks first hand in 2008, but some people are venturing back into equities again. Yet, most people can get the money they need for retirement without gambling heavily on stocks. So, why are they getting back into stocks?

Perhaps these investors have been told that there is no way to make up the losses they suffered, or maybe their looming retirement is causing them to feel there is no more need to worry, since the risk posed by stocks diminishes the longer one holds them. While the desire to get back what one lost is understandable, it is important not to allow this to cloud judgment. Behavioral economics clearly shows that this can cause you to take on more risk than you can handle.

ZviBodie, Professor of Management at Boston University, claims that in spite of the assurances of Wall Street, stocks are always a risky investment, and the longer you hold them, the better your chances of being blindsided by a sudden downturn. While this flies in the face of what many believe, it is actually quite sound.

So, how can you mitigate this risk? Usually this is done through diversification, proper allocation and a disciplined approach to rebalancing. Even this approach holds no guarantees, because investments do not always behave the way we want. Dr. Bodie says that a safer away to build and protect retirement assets is to picture your goal as clearly as possible, then cut things back to the basics, figure out the bare bones level of income you need and invest in products that guarantee this amount, like protected bonds or annuities.

Once you have done this, you can use the rest of your investment money to build reserves to fund your aspirations. You can also limit downside risk through direct purchase of options. Mutual funds that use complex hedging strategies are another choice. These funds are not as transparent, however, and often are much more expensive. Like stocks, they may not work the way you expect, so once again you have not eliminated your risks.

So what are we saying? Unless you put all of your money in annuities, a move we would not recommend, you are going to have some risk in your portfolio.

The bottom line is that there is no risk free investment. You must decide how much of this risk you are willing to take on, but you need to decide with the right information. Stocks do not become less risky over long time horizons. There have been 20 year periods of time where stocks have been flat, and 30-year periods of time where bonds have outperformed them. We are in one of those periods now, and the last one was in 1861. What will the next 150 years look like? Will the next 10 years look like the past 10? Nobody knows. You simply cannot predict what stocks, or any other investment for that matter, will do.

So how should you approach your portfolio? First, you need to forget the idea of catching up. Instead, have a clear picture of your destination, and focus on what you absolutely need. Then, protect yourself from missing the essentials if markets fall short. This is the Summit Wealth way, and we believe it works well for our clients. Instead of trying to recoup losses, which is like doubling down in Las Vegas, you are focusing on making sure you have what you need.

Once you have done this, separate your basic must-have needs from your goals and desires. Set up a sound investment plan that reaches those basics while accounting for inflation through safe investments. Then, add to that as you can.

With a few lucky exceptions, no one gets rich in the stock market. Your investments are probably riskier than you think. As a wealth management firm, the focus we have for our clients is to preserve purchasing power, protect families, and protect against inflation, rising health care costs and taxes. We strive for solid growth through safely managed investment strategies and trusted advice.

Passive Investing

Now that we have seen how your investments are likely riskier than you think, it is time to look at why passive investing is the most active way to assure reliable, predictable, and consistent market-based returns.

Current financial markets are reeling, and Europe and the U.S. are in considerable debt. Insider trading and other stories of fraud have been the headlines of late, while the Federal Reserve has worked to drive down interest rates, a plan that could backfire. In spite of all of this news, the stock markets are up. Passive investing is the reason.

Rather than relying on the investor to chase promising stocks, a broadly diversified, properly allocated and actively rebalanced (passive) portfolio simply works slowly but surely to passively replicate the holdings of the world's greatest companies. This prevents the investor from making poor decisions based on a fluctuating market and eliminates the risks of stock picking, which is rarely successful.

"This is no 'magic black box' technique. This is an approach to investing backed by more than fifty years of academic research and the efforts of Nobel Prize Laureates."

A properly built passive portfolio can save approximately four percent a year. Use the Center for Research and Security Pricing at the University of Chicago (CRSP), and you can further reduce compulsory trading for any index fund that adopts them as benchmarks. These are the types of portfolios we have been recommending for years, and now, people are seeing that they work. They have low net expense ratios, low internal trading, and low taxation. By using passive investments like these, we can strive to help you avoid the loss of four percent a year, year in and year out. This is far more valuable than chasing winners, which may or may not be successful. With passive investing, you can save tremendously over a lifetime of investing.

Jack Bogle's Approach

One of the investment "gurus" we often quote is Jack Bogle. He is the man who started the Vanguard family of mutual funds, whose aim was passive investing in a prudent mix of diversification – never trying to beat the markets, merely attempting to be in the market. In a recent interview, Bogle stated his thoughts that today is the most difficult time for stocks because very few people talk about the dividends.

When he first started an annual report in 1974, the stock dividend yield was about 6.5%; today, it is under three percent. Moreover, corporations play games with earnings. Operating earnings are always higher than reported earnings after write-offs because corporations are always making poor investment decisions.

With regards to today's two percent dividend yield, Bogle says that our economy grows at about five percent before inflation. We can safely assume that the economy grows at no more than five percent a year over the next 10 years. Add on a dividend, and you can expect the investment returns to be close to seven percent, whereas the long-term return on stocks has been 10%. There is about a one in 15 chance that we will face even more economic problems.

In regards to bonds, Bogle claims that they are the biggest problem facing the financial market today. Bond yields are roughly at three percent for the past 10 years. Bogle would not call this situation a bubble, though, because if you hold onto a bond for 10 years, you will get that three percent.

So, what should investors do? First, don't reach for more than your market return, says Bogle. You could try leveraging or buying commodities in gold, and maybe you will do well, but who really knows? Those alterative investments have no internal return – they are 100% speculation.

When the S&P 500 went down 30%, the average equity mutual fund was down 39%, and the average international fund was down 45%, while the average emerging market fund was down 54%. Our moderate conservative portfolio was down between 5.5 to 17%. These were serious losses.

In an age where almost 40% of mutual funds that existed 10 years ago are gone, how can we capitalize on the wisdom of long-term investing when the odds are almost 1 out of 2 that your fund might not be around at the end of the decade?

The answer is to not pick a mutual fund dependent on its past track record, stock selection or manager selection. Instead, be prudently invested, be well diversified, be properly allocated, and apply discipline to the rebalancing. It turns out, our plan is what Bogle has been advocated for years, and it helps you make great decisions.

Manage Risks, Not Returns

In the end, you need to manage your risks, not your returns. That is because, as we keep saying, it is more powerful to avoid the losses than to pick the winners. So how do we manage the risks instead of the returns? This is simple, yet not easy.

In the broad terms, we diversify. We try to have as many of the 12,500 shares in the world's greatest companies as it takes to construct the optimal portfolio. This is easy to talk about and not always easy to implement. Having the proper allocation of asset classes so that when one goes down, the other goes up, or if one goes down, the other does not go down as much, is incredibly challenging.

In addition, we have to have a discipline in the rebalancing so that we are programmatically and systematically buying low and selling high. This sort of discipline is what makes passive investing work, and is the reason that even a conservative portfolio can be up 80% in a down market decade. That 80% is only a 6.5% compound average annual rate of return, and it never involves picking the winners to bring success.

Is "Safe" Actually More Dangerous?

Michael Jackson was known for his dance, the "Moonwalk," where he looked like he was walking forward but he was actually moving backwards. While this may be a popular thing to do in hip-hop, it is not a good investment move, and sadly far too many investors are doing this by playing it safe.

This is important: Consider for example an investor who has some money in a CD paying two percent. A CD is a low-risk investment, because you are guaranteed that two percent, as low as it is. However, there are some serious, unseen risks in this scenario. If this investor is in the 35% tax bracket, then the interest rate is actually a little less than 1.5%. If we are still in the low inflation rate of two percent, then the investor has lost another .5%. The investor thinks he is moving forward, but he is actually moving backwards.

Money market mutual funds, often considered a "safe" investment, can actually be deceivingly dangerous. In the summer of 2011, the largest money market funds had 45% of their investments in European bank paper, and one major money market mutual fund had over 70% in European bank paper. European banks are now in serious trouble. The $2.7 trillion money market mutual fund industry, according to the SCC, has short term funding sources for individuals and institutions as an alternative to traditional bank deposits. In other words, there may not be money to back the promises.

This actually happened a few years ago when one money market fund, the Reserve Primary Fund actually broke the buck, with funds dropping below $1 a share. The SCC is concerned that the mutual money market industry may be headed this way. Recent changes in industry standards make these risks less likely, yet they are risks nonetheless, making a so-called "safe" investment a little less safe than you might think.

So, while you may be using money market funds to lower your risk and protect your investment, you may be on a little riskier ground than you once thought. Those funds may not be backed by any collateral and may be relying on the highly volatile European market. By knowing this, you are empowered to make great decisions.

Investment versus Asset Protection

Over the years, we have found that many investors, when facing challenging economic times, go into protection mode. They begin seeing their investments failing and they want to take steps to protect the assets they have. They take the "just don't lose it" view of investing, focusing all of their concerns on preserving capital, and forgetting about making wealth grow. We believe this is a mistake.

As we have said before, there is no "magic wand" to protect your assets. The people who make it big in the stock market are typically the ones who are just really lucky, or the ones who manage the funds. For instance, a guy who bought into a company at $3 a share when it went public, and sold later at $100 a share will make millions. Those who stick it out with the same company hoping for even greater returns may watch it slide all the way back down to $4 a share. Either the first guy could tell the future, or he got really lucky.

So, how do we help our clients protect their existing assets? Once again, through teaching them to diversify, properly allocate and apply a disciplined approach to rebalancing. Yes, the steps to protect your assets are the same steps to reducing risk, which makes sense. After all, your assets are what are at risk if you take on too much risk.

As you invest, pay attention to the costs, fees and taxes. Get all of the "must know" facts before you make a risk decision. Depend on trusted advice to avoid all of the myths and misconceptions out there.

We view preserving capital as a secondary goal. Wealth building and preserving your future purchasing power, these are actually the primary purposes. After all, you are investing for the long haul, not the immediate future. The typical retiree is looking at 30 years of retirement, and they need to be certain that there is enough money to cover their expenses, as well as leave something for their heirs. With our help, you can do just that, and often end up protecting your assets as well.

The Danger of Leverage

As you look at investing, you must address leverage. We believe that leverage can quickly become an investment mistake. Borrowing to increase the potential return on your investment is very risky. When that investment does not bring the return you anticipated, you are left with nothing but debt.

Yet, when it's done right, leveraging can work well. That is what makes it so dangerous. Investors can make an argument for it when it is done right, but this is a rare occurrence.

Sadly, leveraging has permeated our financial structure to the point of collapse. Some financial instruments have been leveraged 100: 1! That is simply crazy.

Everyone seems to be leveraging the wrong way: borrowing the wrong amounts at the wrong times and on the wrong terms, in order to buy the wrong things at the wrong times for the wrong reasons. So many have failed in this – investors, bankers, governments, and consumers. We let it happen, and now we pay the price. Those who avoided this madness are left to bail out the rest.

When you work with us, do not expect us to advise much leverage. We have seen it go poorly far too many times to recommend it as an investment option. Instead, we will focus on building a prudently invested, diverse portfolio that is properly allocated and rebalanced in a disciplined manner. This has worked for our clients time and time again, and it will continue to do so well into the future.

The Seven Factor Model for Prudent Investing:

True Market Portfolios

We utilize and recommend the academically supported and time tested Seven Factor Model™ to consistently, reliably, and predictably achieve market-based returns, which beat average-investor returns by a long shot. We have already discussed a little about fees and costs. Later you will learn more about some of the remaining items in this Seven Factor Model. This approach will not guaranty that your portfolio will beat your neighbor's portfolio this year or next. It is designed to beat all your neighbors' portfolios over the course of your lifetime.

1. Control costs, fees, taxes, expenses and risks
2. Own shares in the world's great companies
3. Emphasize inexpensive companies
4. Emphasize smaller companies
5. Broadly diversify

6. Allocate appropriately
7. Maintain a disciplined approach to rebalancing

This last factor, one of the products of a properly developed Investment Policy Statement, promotes a systematic and programmatic process to buying low and selling high. If you do not have an Investment Policy Statement, get one right away. Almost all institutional investors have one. It is a great way to navigate through the "fog of investing."

The solution works to achieve a well-diversified portfolio, with up to 12,000 of the world's greatest companies available. We properly allocate these within your risk tolerance, time horizon, and purpose for your money. The staying power of this portfolio then relies on Summit's systematic and diligent rebalancing. This is key: constructing the proper and efficient portfolio is one thing – maintaining it is quite another.

In addition to using ETFs or mutual funds, we prefer the institutional structured fund model that complies with the Center for Research of Security Pricing. It has lower turnover, lower transition costs, and lower trading costs. In these funds you do not have to buy high and sell low, as you do with most index funds.

This solution can potentially lower your costs to as low as 0.96%. As a result, Summit clients can save as much as 63%, and that is after their fees are paid! To see how this works, take a look at this chart; the difference is quite dramatic:

Be Well Diversified

The second step in our investment strategy is proper diversification. By diversifying your portfolio, you bring protection for yourself and your future monetary goals. Sadly, in a volatile market, which ours currently is, people drag their money out of banks and investment firms and stick it somewhere they view as safe, with no risk.

This is the equivalent of sticking your money under your mattress. While on paper it may seem like the safest option, because you face no risk, the facts of inflation actually cause the value of this money to shrink. This is why you need to have your money somewhere that it will earn interest, even if the interest amount is relatively small. Diversification, not pulling out, is the answer to protecting yourself from taking on too much risk.

Understanding Diversification

The first step in this process is to define diversification and its purpose. The goal of diversifying is to try to make money in all circumstances, no matter what the market is doing. With diversification, investors can hedge their risks, smoothing out the bumps on the way up when the market falls. It can cost a little money when some aspects of the portfolio do not perform well at certain times; however, the value that diversification provides is well worth this extra cost.

In a way, this is like trying to sell umbrellas and sunglasses. On sunny days, you will sell sunglasses. On rainy days, you will sell umbrellas, but you need both in your inventory to succeed. The umbrellas will not sell well when it is sunny, but they are necessary to get you through the rainy days.

Now, in this scenario, a raincoat does not really diversify your business. It simply extends your rainy day offerings. It does not help on snowy days. Instead, you should add a snowplow to your offerings. That is diversification.

Diversifying refers to adding products to the portfolio that will get you through certain times in the market. Each asset must be unique and fill a unique need for your investment plan.

An asset class must meet these three criteria:

1. Be compositionally unique (unlike the umbrella and raincoat)
2. Be compositionally stable (the raincoat cannot morph into a snowplow)
3. Have low correlation – it goes up when the other asset classes go down (the raincoat and the umbrella move in unison, whereas the sunglasses and the umbrella move in opposite directions)

In investing, asset classes include:

- Debts (bonds, convertibles, preferred shares, fixed income
- Equity (stocks, equity mutual funds)
- Cash
- Commodities (real estate, gold, oil, and similar products)

Some argue that insurance should be included as a fifth asset class. This could be included, but over-diversification is a common problem, so we prefer to stick with the four mentioned above.

1973 - 2010

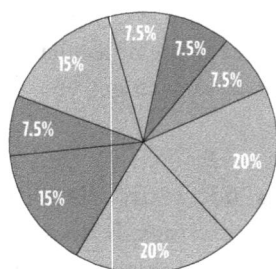

	Annualized Return (%)	Annualized Standard Deviation (%)
Portfolio 1	3.83	19.79
Portfolio 2	9.81	18.53
Portfolio 3	9.26	11.66
Portfolio 4	9.33	11.70
Portfolio 5	10.49	12.49
Portfolio 6	10.99	12.12

	Equity Mutual Funds	S&P 500 Index	5 - Year Government Portfolio	One - Year Fixed Income	EAFE Index	U.S. 9 - 10 Small Co.	Int'l Small Cap Stocks	U.S. Small Cap Value	U.S. Large Cap Value
Portfolio 1	100%								
Portfolio 2		100%							
Portfolio 3		60%	20%	20%					
Portfolio 4		30%	20%	20%	30%				
Portfolio 5		15%	20%	20%	15%	15%	15%		
Portfolio 6		7.5%	20%	20%	15%	7.5%	15%	7.5%	7.5%

* Portfolio 1 - Data from DALBAR, Inc. Quantitive Analysis of Investor Behavior, 2011, 1990 - 2010.
Return and Standard Deviation data from DFA Returns Software updated through 12/31/10.
Past Performance is no guarantee of future results. Asset Allocation and diversification strategies cannot insure a profit or protect against a loss.

The Need for Diversification

Why do we need to diversify? Frankly, because no one can predict reliably and consistently which asset category will perform well this year or next, or even this decade or the next decade. No matter how skilled someone may become at picking the winners, there is still some luck involved in the process. Diversifying protects against this. If one asset doesn't do well, the others will balance it out.

The actions of the market are outside of our control, but diversification is in our control. We cannot say whether or not it will rain, so we keep an umbrella in the car. We cannot predict whether or not it will be hot, so we keep a hat to protect our head if the sun is out. This is the same philosophy that we use in diversification. We cannot predict what the market will do, so we gather a mix of assets to protect against all possibilities.

Our current financial crisis likely took everything you thought you knew about calibrating investment risk and turned it on its head. This can be an unsettling situation, and we want to caution you that it is not likely to flip back tomorrow.

The crucial question all investors face is this: "What is risky and what is safe?" With the changes in what you know, everything you once thought was safe and dull turned out to be dangerous, and the more risky options turned out to be quite reliable.

This points to the reason for diversification. You, or your current advisor, may think you know what is safe, but as recent trends have shown, you could be completely wrong. What would happen to your portfolio if what you thought were true was not? Would you be protected today, or in serious trouble?

Remember, no investment is risk free. We cannot stress this strongly enough. Yet, unscrupulous advisors are always going to try to sell you on a "safe" investment. In the end, someone who professes to know which way these asset classes will go is either lying to you or lying to himself. Either way, your future is at stake. It is only through proper diversification that you can build some protection into your portfolio.

What *Not* to Do in Diversifying

Diversifying can be a bit tricky, and we have seen many people doing it in a poor way. Sadly, the advice most people get from television pundits and their interviewees is less than ideal.

1973 - 2010

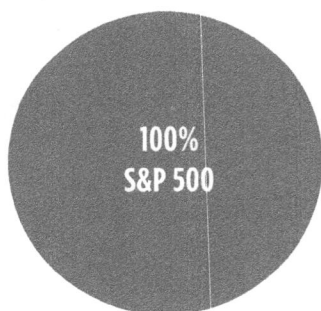

	Annualized Return (%)	Annualized Standard Deviation (%)
Portfolio 1	3.83	19.79
Portfolio 6	9.81	18.53

100% S&P 500

	Equity Mutual Funds	S&P 500 Index
Portfolio 1	100%	
Portfolio 2		100%

* Portfolio 1 - Data from DALBAR, Inc. Quantitive Analysis of Investor Behavior, 2011, 1990 - 2009. Return and Standard Deviation data from DFA Returns Software updated through 12/31/09. Past Performance is no guarantee of future results. Asset Allocation and diversification strategies cannot insure a profit or protect against a loss.

One of the ways people "diversify" is to open a brokerage account or retirement fund, then deposit their money into the top performing assets at the time, maybe choosing 10 to 30 of these as recommended by the financial press. Ten years later, this same investor owns around 10 to 30 mutual funds or similar assets. This may feel diverse, but it actually is not. If the investor looks closely, he probably has way too many of the same stock tucked away in different funds.

How does this happen? If there is a stock performing particularly well, the fund manager wants to look good, so he may choose to "window dress" the portfolio to make it appear that he did not miss this stock.

This often leads to the stock being purchased after the price increases. The manager has followed the herd chasing the winners. The fund becomes distorted, too large and over diversified. A lack of an Investment Policy Statement or investing philosophy leads to a fund that is too big, inefficient, expensive, and riddled with gaps and redundancies. This is not quality diversification.

Under diversification can also be problematic. When large segments of investors try to purchase the same assets and do the same thing, they concentrate, rather than spread, their risk. When they see others making a lot of money in one particular asset class, they pour all of their money into that fund. In the end, their risk is all tied up in one particular product, which will eventually have a downward trend.

Remember, those assets that are performing poorly right now are likely to come back. Stocks, equities, and whatever other investment option you have in mind typically do come back. We may not be able to see how this will happen, and it may not happen fast enough for our comfort, but it is likely to happen. When investors start escaping from these poorly performing assets, they are setting themselves up for the mistake of under-diversification.

Remember, the funds that are doing poorly now will come back, and the funds that are doing well now may be poised for a crash. With a trusted advisor you will never be able to invest so much in any one asset that you make a killing. This is a good thing, because you will never invest so much that you get killed, either. Only proper diversification can protect you from these dangers.

Bees and Manatees

What can we learn from bees and manatees? Consider a story that happened to one of our financial advisors, as told in his own words.

My house at the beach has a long 400 foot driveway with tropical foliage. Every Saturday morning when I'm there I make it my business to put out the American flag.

This time, however, I stepped on a hornet's nest, and I didn't realize it at first but there must have been 200, 300, maybe 400 of these hornets buzzing around my lower leg to the point where I jumped out of my flip flops and ran down the shell driveway.

My feet were hurting. I must have been stung at least five or six times. In one instance I could actually see the stinger continuing to pump venom into my skin as I plucked it out. I still have patch of skin on my arm that is looking pretty nasty.

I walked... rather, I trotted all the way back to the house across the coquina shell driveway, put on another pair of shoes and went back to try to salvage my flip flops, but that required me finding a stick that was 10 feet long. I couldn't get anywhere near where I had planted the flag because the bees were hyper-alert.

I finally made it back to the house where I received little sympathy from my wife. Fortunately, I'm not allergic to bee stings, yet.

A little while later we decided to take a walk along the beach and it was absolutely beautiful, 85 degrees, 10 mile an hour wind, crystal clear turquoise waters. A couple of dolphins swam by, then tarpon. We could see someone snorkeling along the shore, Osprey overhead, oyster catchers, pelicans, sea gulls, the works.

About 15 minutes into our walk, we noticed this large brown patch in the beautiful crystal clear water moving ever so slowly. It was a pod of manatees (it's manatee mating season). It looked like a mother and two calves, though it might have been too early in the season. They could have been mating. I don't know. But it's rare to see manatees even though our house is in Manatee County. I can count the number of times in the 17 years we've lived here that I've seen manatees and yet we see dolphin several times a day. One of the cows must have been at least 10, 12, 14 feet long. She was huge and lumbering so slowly and only 30 feet offshore."

The point of this story is that diversity in nature has a purpose. The manatees are huge and slow and rare. The bees are tiny and fast and there are hundreds of them in tight quarters. Both fulfill an important role in the balance of nature, even with their differences.

We should apply this same principle found in nature to our investment portfolios. Nature does not have diversity for diversity's sake, but diversity to diversify. We should all have the occasional manatee in our portfolio, as well as all of the bees that our portfolio requires, in the proper allocation and with a disciplined approach to rebalancing. This will ensure that we never have more manatees than we have bees. Remember, too many manatees and too few bees could lead to ecological disaster. In the same way, an unbalanced portfolio is a financial disaster waiting to happen.

Proper Diversification

We have looked at how not to diversify, but what strategies are sound diversification strategies? A diverse portfolio will be a blend of stocks, bonds, bills and notes, and commodities. Mutual funds also play a role in the diverse portfolio, and some people will have nothing more than these as their investment because they are already diversified and are monitored by the mutual fund manager. Even though mutual funds are already diverse, this is not proper diversification because it relies too heavily on one investment form. Also, these mutual funds may actually overlap, offering you multiple shares off the very same stocks.

So what is proper diversification? Proper diversification requires a portfolio with a balance between high-yield, high-risk assets and low-yield, low risk assets. This allows your investments to make your money commitment worthwhile, while providing a cushion of protection that keeps it from all disappearing on a few terrible market days.

As you diversify, you need to keep your level of risk tolerance in mind. Risk tolerance is the level of fluctuation you can handle over any given period of time. This is not an emotional decision, but is a cash decision. It is made based on your purpose for your money.

If your investments will be used to grow an endowment to build a large library at a University in 30 years, that is very different than if your investments are supplementing a pension plan and you know you have payouts coming every single month. If your money is being used for your children's college fund, and they will be heading to school in the next 5 to 15 years, then you will have a different risk tolerance than someone who is looking to use the money to retire in 30 to 35 years.

Proper diversification creates a portfolio with a mix of assets that are properly allocated so that you do not have too much of one and not enough of another. In addition, the proportion is exactly right to meet your goals, match your risk tolerance, fulfill your purpose for the money and stay within your time horizon. This means you will not have just 5 assets as recommended by Kim Dramer, or 30 assets according to the Dow Jones Industrial, or even 500 with the S&P 500 or 2,000 with the Russell 2,000. Instead, we will build it out of 12,000+ shares of the world's greatest companies.

Why the world's greatest companies? Well, in the last 10 years, the number of US companies in which one could invest with any amount of liquidity numbered 8,800. By the middle of 2011, that number was down to 5,100 companies, and yet the number of stocks, mutual funds and ETFs has increased from 25,000 to over 41,000.

What does that tell us? First, there are fewer opportunities to invest in America. Second, there are 44 countries in which anyone would want to be invested, including countries in Europe and Asia as well as Mexico, Israel, South Africa and Canada.

So, how much should we invest in those 44 countries? The US now represents about 30% of the total world wealth, so we advocate approximately 30% of our stock investments should be in US companies. The proportion depends on your risk tolerance, time horizon and purpose for money. In the remaining 43 countries outside the US, there are perhaps another 7000 stocks. Thus, we advocate investing in most, if not all of the 12,000 of the world's great companies. How does that sound for diversification?

Proper Asset Allocation

Proper allocation first requires a true understanding of what defines an asset class. Academically, there are three pre-requisites, which we will discuss in some detail.

They are: 1) Each asset class must be Compositionally Unique; 2) Each asset class must be Compositionally Stable, and; 3) Each asset class must have Relatively Low Correlations.

Compositionally Unique means that they must look and feel the same. Debt structures and Equity structures cannot be in the same asset class. In the first you are a Loaner. In the second, you are an Owner. Nor would a commodity (like orange juice or pork bellies or real estate) belong in the same asset class as cash.

Allocation	
U.S. Large Cap	15%
U.S. Small Cap	5%
International	7%
Emerging Markets	3%
Commodities	3%
Money Market	5%
U.S. Short-term	20%
U.S. Intermediate Bonds	12%
U.S. High Yield	5%
U.S. Long-term Bonds	15%
International Bonds	10%
Total:	100%

Sample Conservative Allocation

Compositionally Stable that means the asset class cannot have lots of different components coming into or flowing out of it to remain an asset class. For example, many of use the Dow Jones Industrial Average, or the S&P (for Standard and Poor's) 500 as the proxie for the asset class of Large U.S. Stocks. However, should we use the Russell 2000 as the proxie for Small U.S. Stocks? The Russell 2000 has an average annual turnover of 38%. It is not stable. (This does not even bring into the discussion as to whether these commercially derived indices are asset classes at all. We prefer the CRSP, pronounced "crisp" model. CRSP stands for the Center for Research in Security Pricing. It is based upon the academic research from the University of Chicago.).

Relatively Low Correlations means that one asset class will not behave like another, too much. They may all go up or down simultaneously, but the relative amounts of correlated valuations should be highly distinguishable. Bonds, which go up in value as interests go down, usually is accompanied by stocks going relatively down in value, and vice versa. If bonds go down, stocks are usually pricier by comparison. What about high-yield corporate bonds (sometimes erroneously referred to as "junk bonds") with their rates of return that are quite similar to the returns experienced by and expected from stocks? These would not be considered a true asset class. They behave similarly.

So there are only 4 agreed upon true asset classes: Stocks, Bonds, Commodities, and Cash. Each has their sub-categories. There is a fifth type of asset that the academics are currently arguing over and exploring to determine if it fulfills the criteria: Insurance products (life and annuities). It is because these are unique, stable and behave independently of all the asset classes.

Money Markets or No Money Markets

Money markets are one asset you could have in your portfolio, and some feel these are a safe option. We have already identified reasons why this is not exactly the case, primarily the fact that these funds are often tied heavily to struggling European banks. With Europe facing a debt crisis, this is a very real cause for concern.

About half of the assets in the 10 largest US prime money market funds are invested in European bank debt. This risk could break the buck easily. This happened in 2008 for the first time in 14 years, and it could easily happen again.

When we look at your portfolio with rebalancing in mind, money markets are one fund we will look at closely. Now, we do not want you to fear these funds. Remember, back in 2008 just one fund broke the buck. Even the European debt crisis does not mean that these funds are guaranteed to fail. As always, you should not make any fast, emotion-based decisions, but you should know that there is more risk than you might think in these funds.

Also, you should know that there is an alternative. You do not have to use money market funds if you are looking for a "safe" asset to add to your portfolio. Short-term U.S. treasuries and certificates of deposits offer similar safety nets, without the European debt risk.

Municipal Bonds

Most people choose to invest in municipal bonds because they want to sleep well. For as far back as anyone can remember, municipal bonds operated with a set it and forget it mentality. There was very little risk with these investments, and the eventual income was fair, if not substantial. Municipal bonds were boring, but the security they brought was beautiful.

This may be changing, however, with ongoing municipal bond problems in major cities like Los Angeles and Chicago, where declining tax revenue, increasing entitlements and politicians who will not make cuts are destroying budgets. Cities are filing Chapter 9 bankruptcy left and right, leaving their investors with nothing.

So is it time to jump ship and forget about municipal bonds altogether? Not necessarily. Some of the best bonds at four percent are maturing in the year 2020. Their recent price had a yield to maturity of 3.5% income. Opportunities like this are excellent for tax deferred, tax free income. While it is true that three, four and five percent rates of return are nothing to write home about, but remember, those rates are tax free. That makes them more like five to eight percent in today's tax rates. Not too shabby.

With the right municipal bond, you can still bring in a decent amount of income. You simply need the right information to make this decision.

Gold as a Commodity

As you look at disciplined rebalancing, you must consider what investments will be in your portfolio. When markets start to struggle, worried investors often wonder if they would be better off investing in a commodity such as gold.

Everybody is talking about gold. When gold broke the $1,500 an ounce mark, you couldn't turn on the TV, visit the Internet or read the newspaper without seeing some person talking about gold. This makes the investor want to jump into the frenzy with both feet. We often advise our investors to use caution when investing in gold in the current market, and here's why:

- We're late to the party. Gold is already at extremely high prices
- Fundamentals may not justify the prices. There is no real demand for the metal in today's markets either for industrial purposes or for jewelry.
- When the economy improves, gold could fizzle
- You may already own enough gold. If you have a diverse portfolio, your level of gold exposure is probably already appropriate. Just like any other investment, gold could go down, or it could continue to increase. Adding more may not make sense.

- Gold is not a good inflation hedge. Gold is a good store of value in times of turmoil, but oil has been a better inflation hedge over the past two decades.
- Gold has no intrinsic value. It produces no income. It employs no one. It has a high cost for storage and insurance.

Do we believe you should own gold? Yes, we do, and most of our clients have some in their portfolios. The question really is how much you should own. Our philosophy is "just the right amount." That amount will depend on your risk tolerance, purpose for money and time horizon.

When you hear people touting gold as a good protecting investment, be realistic. Remember, there are five risks that could impact your portfolio. These are: inflation, deflation and economic stagnation, investment fees, taxes, and health costs. Gold only insulates from one of these, at most, and that is inflation. It is not the best inflation hedge, but it can provide some protection.

Over the past 100 years, gold has delivered a net return, net of inflation, of about one percent per year. Subtract holding costs and you get a half a point a year or so. That's no way to retire comfortably. Gold should only be a part of your investment portfolio, not what you are banking your retirement on completely.

Real Estate as an Investment

Is real estate a solid investment? To decide, you need to take a look at the history of real estate as an investment. If you do, you will find a long and deep history of periodic bankruptcies among real estate developers. Is there a reason to think that your investments will be more successful than these professionals?

Real estate is not a sure thing. It is all about being lucky in your timing. If you are unlucky, you will lose money, and you can lose a lot of money.

The fact is no one knows when, or even if, real estate is going to rebound. The industry faces $5 trillion in commercial mortgages that have to be refinanced in the next two to five years, and these have reduced loan to value ratios, higher debt to income ratios and reduced income and pricing structures.

So what does this mean? Many are going to be paying out of pocket for their refinance or finding ways to provide greater collateral amounts. This decreases the attraction of real estate. When real estate is not attractive, prices are driven down. Like gold, real estate can, and maybe should, be a part of your investment portfolio, but you need to have the discipline to sell when necessary, even at a loss. Also, this asset class needs to be just a limited portion of your portfolio, not the majority of it.

Stocks... Thinly Traded Please

We all know that the small investor rarely has the edge on Wall Street, but this does not mean that stocks should be shunned altogether. Roger Ibbotson says that thinly traded stocks could be an exception. See, the Fama-French three-factor model shows that you must have some stocks in order to achieve quality returns. Ibbotson's philosophy about thinly traded stocks is in line with this.

The model states that:

- Stocks are necessary in order to achieve quality returns
- Those stocks should be value stocks with a low book to price
- They should be smaller, or thinly traded stocks

We believe in a fourth factor, trusted advice, to ensure that the stocks you buy are inline with your goals. Also, that trusted advisor should help you set up your rebalancing plan so that it systematically, programmatically and automatically buys low and sells high.

Remember, you cannot beat the markets. In fact, of the 250 largest endowments and foundations, over 85% do not meet their own blended benchmarks, even before paying their investment consultant fees. For instance, the Ford Foundation is the largest of these with approximately $13.5 billion. They have not met their goals. If $13.5 billion is not enough to beat the markets, what would be?

We believe that you should not even try to beat the markets. Instead, focus on the four-step approach: prudent investing, diversification, allocation and disciplined rebalancing, and you will do well. Thinly traded stocks should be part of this model.

Now that you know what makes an asset class, how do apportion, or allocate these among your portfolio? Prudent investing and proper diversification are followed by proper allocation. Asset allocation and diversification go hand in hand. Diversification means creating a portfolio with multiple assets, and allocation refers to the strategy used to balance the risk and reward of those assets, choosing the right combination so that your goals, risk tolerance and investment horizon are all taken into consideration.

Five Common Asset Allocation Myths

Selecting your asset classes to manage risk and capture returns is a very delicate process. All too often, myths in the industry push investors into making poor decision. Knowing what these myths are will help you avoid the dangerous practices associated with them.

Myth One: "Asset allocation protects you from the bear"

Asset allocation cannot protect you from all losses. No matter what you put into your portfolio, some of your investments will fail! You must be willing to accept this risk. What asset allocation can do is provide you with a reasonable amount of security. For instance, if one asset class goes down 60% and another asset class goes down by only five percent, and both are in your portfolio, then the average of these losses makes your portfolio go down by only 32.5%.

Myth Two: "Tactical asset allocation is best in a volatile market"

Tactical asset allocation refers to trying to choose some of the assets in your portfolio based on how you think they will perform. In other words, you might choose to overweight your portfolio with Japanese assets because you believe Japan will "do better" this year.

This concept is nothing more than market timing in disguise. Prudent, market-based investors avoid tactical asset allocation in any way, shape or form, as it is nothing more than speculating and gambling.

Myth Three: "There is an optimal strategic asset allocation"

Simply stated, there is not. There is, however, historical evidence of asset class performance derived from sophisticated mathematical models that we can use to base our decisions. We cannot predict the future, but we can use history to give greater clarity to our decision making.

Myth Four: "Constant rebalancing is needed"

Rebalancing is vital to prevent your portfolio from taking on too much risk or failing to have appropriate rates of return. Periodic rebalancing is important. However, rebalancing too frequently is problematic because of the cost. Every time you rebalance, there are fees involved. That is why we believe in a disciplined approach to rebalancing.

Myth Five: "More funds equal greater diversification"

This is, perhaps, the greatest myth of them all. When people come to us for our free market investment analysis, they are often amazed to see how much asset overlap is in their supposedly diverse portfolios.

In fact, we had one client who was surprised to see that he held 17 different accounts with 30 different mutual funds and, lo and behold, they included 60 different stocks that were held by five different mutual funds. That is not diversification. It is over concentration, which is highly ineffective and very costly.

Do not fall prey to these five common myths. Perfection does not exist in investing or in asset allocation. Instead, you need to focus on proper asset allocation by developing a diversified portfolio from over 12,000 stocks in more than 42 countries. This can yield substantial gains, and this is our asset allocation strategy for most of our clients. With it, you can meet your investment goals with your acceptable amount of risk on your time horizon.

Asset Allocation Mistakes to Avoid

One common allocation mistake is frequently changing your asset allocations. This is the mark of an investor without a clear investment strategy or proper Investment Policy Statement. Before you begin building your portfolio, a leading firm will help you define your goals and parameters, then design a portfolio around those. Occasional disciplined rebalancing may be necessary, yet constantly changing our asset allocation is not the answer. Stay strong to stay rich.

Tactical asset allocation is another dangerous mistake, as we said before. Trying to time the markets is, simply, risky and dangerous. In bull markets, investors become too aggressive, overweighting stocks beyond their risk based on the Markowitz Efficient Frontier. This leads to taking on too much risk for too little gain.

Now, it's easy to look smart when all stocks go up. It's easy to get lulled into a false sense of security. Your success leads to the false conclusion that what happened recently is likely to continue. This is what makes market timing so dangerous.

Just because the last 20 years or 50 years or even the last 200 years have benefited stock investors over bond investors does not mean that the trend will continue. It seems likely that it will, but predictions are difficult to make, especially about the future. Then, in bear markets, investors become too conservative. Some even go to cash well after the portfolio value has dropped. Instead of protecting themselves, they actually lock in their losses with this action. Usually, investors get out too late, and then the problems with this become compounded by getting in too late.

Market timing rarely works well. "Tactical Asset Allocation" is just a fancy name for market timing. You can pay someone extra for this, but remember, they have the same 50% chance of being correct as anyone else. Sadly, those who practice this form of asset allocation only outperform the index about 15% of the time.

Math Is Not Money

As you decide where to allocate your investments, remember, math is not money. Do not allow yourself to be fooled by what you see. Often, you find yourself tempted to invest in a fund because of its seemingly consistent track record, but this could be problematic.

For example, take ProFundsUtra Nasdaq-100. This fund has trounced the vast majority of its peers that invest in large blue-chip stocks in three of the past four years. Its annual return report shows that in 2007 it earned 28% and was in the top four percent of its peers. In 2008 it lost 73%, which was in the bottom one percent of its peers. Then, in 2009 it earned 188%, and in 2010 it earned 11%.

Now, on the surface that fund looks like it has a 21% average annual rate of return for four years. Unfortunately, had you started out with $100 in 2007, you would only wind up with $94. See how this works:

Say there is a financial Mensa out there who can take your $100 and earn 100% the first year, but loses 60% the next year, and therefore has a 40% rate of return over two years. If that person could be guaranteed of getting you a 30% return, you would probably want to sign up.

Unfortunately, this math is deceiving. If you started out with $100 and went up 100% the first year, you would have $200. If you went down 60% the second year, you would have lost $120, because 60% of 200 is 120. Therefore, you now only have $80. Thus, your 20% guaranteed rate of return lost you $20. Now, to take the $80 back to $200, you would need to have a 150% return, and that is incredibly unlikely.

Example number two is the CGM Focus Fund, the fund that ended as the number one mutual fund on December 31, 2009. This fund earned an annual average return of about 22%. Unfortunately, the average investor earned a negative 11%. How can that possibly be?

Or consider this: If you look at a chart of XYZ Company and flipped a coin 60 times in a row, you would see that the stock doubled over a 60 day period of time, simply by flipping a coin. This was actually done by Burton Malkiel in his book *A Random Walk Down Wall Street*.

Math			Money		
					Value
Time	Return		Time	Return	$1,000,000
Year 1	100%		Year 1	100%	$2,000,000
Year 2	-60%		Year 2	-60%	$1,200,000
Total	40%		Total		$800,000
	÷ 2 years =+20% (Average Annual Rate of Return)				= $200,000 loss (+150%)

What is the point of this discussion? When you are trying to choose the assets you will have in your portfolio, it is impossible to determine which ones are going to outperform this year or the next. In fact, sometimes strong performance can still equal losses for investors. Because of this, you are always better off choosing a range of asset classes and working to avoid the losses. Do not get burned. Make great decisions.

Disciplined Re-balancing

Buy and hold does not work. Buy and rebalance is the key. Managing a portfolio requires periodic, disciplined rebalancing. Sometimes, there are simply assets that need to be sold and new ones that need to be acquired. However, this should never be done in a reactionary, emotional way.

We advocate methodical, planned rebalancing that avoids emotional decisions and favors rational, evidence-based ones. The way to accomplish this is through a written Investment Policy Statement (or IPS). Institutional Investors would not consider investing without an IPS. The IPS tells us what and when to buy and when to sell, and how much.

It is the plan for investing. Do not invest without one. It is like flying a plane without a flight plan, or operating on a cataract without an organized process. You would not want your eye surgeon making erratic, emotional surgical decisions. You should not want your investment advisor, even if you try (and too often fail) to do it yourself to attempt investing without an IPS. Have and use and refer to your IPS frequently. This is the way to ensure that you programmatically, systematically, and automatically buy low and sell high.

Why Rebalance? Even Warren Buffett Does!

Warren Buffett is arguably the most famous investor in history, and he recently announced the need to reshuffle his holdings. So what does this tell us? Even the "best investor in history" makes mistakes or has assets that do not perform as he expected. If that's the case, chances are the rest of us will too. You may never get as famous as Warren Buffett, but with our prudent model, you can be certain that you achieve market base returns reliably, consistently and predictably.

As we look at disciplined rebalancing, it is helpful to take a closer look at some of the assets you could have in your portfolio, along with their benefits and drawbacks. We will also discuss some poor strategies for rebalancing, and what you, with the help of your advisor, should do instead.

Investing in a Volatile Market

While we have thoroughly explained our investment strategy and its four points, we feel it is important to address the current market volatility and how it affects our investment plans. This will help you understand why Summit Wealth is a trustworthy place for your assets, even in these challenging economic times.

Dealing with Volatility

Nobody likes when the market goes down, but everyone has to tackle this problem. We believe it is best to control your emotions when facing periodic downside volatility. This is simply part of the market, and you cannot get the longer-term average returns common in the markets without a downward trend from time to time. Downward trends are the flip side of the upward trends. We fear the downs, but love the ups. However, we cannot have one without the other. They are two sides of the same coin of investing. Like risk and return. You cannot have one without the other.

You may hear some investment "gurus" tell you that you can get the upside without periodic downside volatility. This is false. These individuals are preying on your wish fulfillment and emotional attachment to money. No one, no matter how much they try to make you think they can, can predict the short-term actions of the market.

Remember, when we build your portfolio, we are looking to create something that will bring returns for the long-term, even beyond your lifetime if you wish, not in the next six months. It is vital that you do not allow short-term volatility to drive your behavior. This will lead to long-term underperformance, which is costly.

Why is this part of our discussion of rebalancing? Because we need you to understand that we have a plan to deal with market volatility. We will rebalance your portfolio when needed to help counter changes in the market. Diversification allows us to take rebalance assets easily when one, such as stocks, is down, without rebalancing too often in reaction to the market.

As you can see, our four-fold approach to investing, investing prudently, building a diverse portfolio, focusing on proper asset allocation and taking a disciplined approach to rebalancing, makes sense. Instead of trying to beat the markets, we try to use them to avoid losses and improve your bottom line, ensuring you do not run out of fumes when you are in retirement. With Summit Wealth, you will have the information that you need to make great decisions.

What You Really Want from Your Investments

We have discussed how the Seven Factor Model™ approach to investing brings stable and reliable returns. Yet, many people still find themselves chasing the dream of beating the market. They find themselves investing in exotic options like foreign currency in order to try to create above market returns. Yet, this has a serious flaw.

Consider investing in a foreign currency. If you think that the Japanese yen is going to have an advantage over the American dollar, you may try to sell dollars and buy yens. If you are right, you could do well, but this works much like a tennis game. You have an opponent on the other side. You're on one side of the net thinking that the yen will go up, and your opponent is on the other side thinking that it will go down. One of you will lose.

Have you considered who is on the other side of the net? Is the yen seller someone like Goldman Sachs, The Bank of Tokyo or Mitsubishi? What do they know that you don't know? What do you know that they don't know? There is more to investing than just picking a winner.

In the end, you need to define what you really want from your investments. Often, what we want from our investments is directly related to how we think and feel about them. We spend our time trying to cajole the markets to give us what we want, even though that is as ridiculous as it sounds.

We all want high returns from our investments. We want to nurture our hopes for riches and banish our fear of poverty. We want to beat the market, and we want to feel pride when our investments bring gains, avoiding the regret that comes with losses. We want the status and esteem of hedge funds, the warm glow and virtue of socially responsible funds and the patriotism of investing in our own country. We want good advice from financial advisors and media gurus. We want to be free from government regulations, yet protected by the government at the same time. We want to leave a legacy for our children when we're gone, with nothing for the tax man.

It is these wants and the resulting behaviors that make financial markets go up or down. When we herd together, we create bubbles. When we go our separate ways, we pop them. What ends up happening is giving more weight to the investment than its main purpose. The main purpose of investing is to own shares in the world's greatest companies so you can participate in their profits and enjoy the benefits of that profit. When we start attributing more to our investments than that, we set ourselves up for problems.

Remember, your investments do not love you. You need to avoid loving them. It is common for there to be emotional attachments to investments, but you must remember that an investment is nothing more than owning a share in a company that should provide profit.

How can you avoid giving in to these emotional attachments to your money? You do so by making sound decisions with the help of trusted financial advice.

No one can predict the future; at least not reliably and consistently. No one should try. That is one of the easiest ways to achieve a small fortune – once you start with a large fortune. The signs of gambling and speculating are: stock picking, market timing, and track record chasing, and these are based upon the myth that someone has superior skill in predicting the future. True, some can and do beat the markets. The trouble is, they cannot do it for the long haul, and it is impossible to identify them in advance.

REPEAT after me "AVOID Gambling and Speculating". It is a portfolio killer. The signs include: Stock-Picking, Market-Timing, Track Record-Chasing. Market-timing can go by many names, such as Dynamic Portfolio Modeling, Tactical Asset Allocation, Sector Rotation, Strategic Asset Allocation. "A rose is a rose..." More to the point, a skunk is a skunk.

Rather remember and employ the three hallmarks of PRUDENT INVESTING. The signs of prudent investing are simple: diversify, allocate, re-balance.

The previous is worth repeating and remembering. Again repeat after me: "Prudent Investing requires you to:

1. Diversify broadly
2. Allocate properly, and
3. Re-Balance, using a disciplined approach"

Seven Factor Model™ in Review

We utilize and recommend the academically supported and time tested Seven Factor Model™ to consistently, reliably, and predictably achieve market-based returns, which beat average investor returns by a long shot. This approach will not guaranty that your portfolio will beat your neighbor's portfolio this year or next. It is designed to beat all your neighbors' portfolios over the course of your lifetime:

1. Control costs, fees, taxes, expenses and risks
2. Own shares in the world's great companies
3. Emphasize inexpensive companies
4. Emphasize smaller companies
5. Broadly diversify
6. Allocate appropriately
7. Use a disciplined approach to rebalance

This last factor, a product of your Investment Policy Statement, promotes a systematic, automatic, programmatic way to buy low and sell high. If you do not have an Investment Policy Statement, get one right away. Almost all institutional investors have one. It is the way to navigate through the fog of investing.

Key Takeaways
- Have an Investment Policy Statement
- Get *all most know facts before* making a decision
- Seek consistent excellence, not occasional brilliance
- Mange risks, rather than returns
- There is no "magic black box" for successful investing
- Utilize the Seven Factor Model™
- Passive investing offers the most active path to reliable, predictable, and consistent market-based returns

Chapter 6: How to Live off your Nest Egg, without Killing the Golden Goose

"Attitude is a little thing that makes a big difference."

–Winston Churchill

Distributing

Setting aside enough to live out your retirement as you plan is just the first step in enjoying your golden years. You also need to plan for distributing those funds. Sadly, this is where many investors who have been planning properly mess up. Without the right distribution plan, you could end up paying out much of what you have saved in unnecessary taxes, whether when you take the money for retirement or when you leave it to your heirs.

Trickle or Torrent

When it comes to your retirement, you have two basic options: have a trickle of money coming each month, or a raging torrent. With proper planning and positioning help, you can enjoy the latter.

Did you know that a considerable amount of your money could be earning zero percent? Are the bulk of those funds in an account with heavy withdrawal restrictions? Would it make sense to put the rest of your retirement savings into a vehicle where the government tells you how much to put in, when you can take it out, and then shares in the profits and not the losses?

Do you have contacts to help you get your Social Security payments in a lump sum and tax free? Has anyone shown you how to do this? There are also methods to take money out of your 401(k) tax free and still leave the 401(k) to your heirs. These are some ways to harness the power of inflation, rather than be hindered by it. As you've noticed, there are ways to reduce your risk and invest like a pro, while cutting fees and lowering overall costs. In the end, a leading wealth management firm can help you discover how you can have an effective increased rate of return by identifying inefficiencies (money you are unknowingly losing), stopping the leaks, recapturing the funds, and putting back into positive action.

Planning for Retirement

Retirement income planning, for most of us, was pretty much a theoretical exercise 25 years ago. Now, this is not the case. Rather than being mainly concerned with cumulating assets, we now have to be concerned about maintaining an income stream, keeping up with inflation and never running out of money.

H. L. Makin said this succinctly, "For every complex problem there is an answer that is clear, simple and wrong." Here are some truths that should guide your retirement planning:

In the real world, there is no such thing as a straight line or a smooth curve. Portfolio performance and client behavior go hand in hand. Many clients, unfortunately, make the wrong move or are unfortunately lucky at the wrong time.

Also, there is no such thing as a safe investment. Every investment has risk, although some have more than others. Retirement planning demands obsessive scrutiny of risk. We endeavor to better educate our clients as to all the possible risks in their portfolios. Remember, performance alone won't achieve retirement success. You also need to avoid unnecessary losses.

We also need to look at human nature when planning for retirement. For example, we are not wired to conceptualize large sums of capital. This is why so many lottery winners file for bankruptcy just a short time after winning, and also why so many highly paid athletes cannot make ends meet. Humans also have little capacity to predict their spending patterns five years from now, let alone 40.

Finally, the answer to successful retirement is not relying on one "simple" solution or product. Remember what Makin said? The simple solution is almost always wrong. Retirement income planning is more about the process then the product. You need a structured income protection system, and we can help create it.

Attitudes Toward Retirement

Surveys regularly show that attitudes toward retirement today are surprisingly positive. Consider these highlights:

54% of people view retirement as a "new chapter" in life, rather than a winding down. This is a significant increase over the 38% that held a similar view in 2000.

Pre-retirement is being postponed. Retirees now say they intend to delay retirement by at least five years, from 64 to 69. This is in part triggered by increasing longevity as well as the financial and economic meltdown.

Retirement no longer means the end of work. Almost two-thirds say they would ideally like to remain productive and include some work in retirement to stay active and involved.

Financial peace of mind is now six times more important than is accumulating wealth. A full 82% named it in their key financial goal.

Yet, a positive attitude is not enough to make your retirement plan successful. You also need the right planning and advice.

According to Ken Dychtwald, author of The Age Wave, "In almost every conceivable way, people who had a financial advisor in their corner turned out far better than people who tried to do it themselves. We asked in a survey if people are displeased with their advisors after what's happened this last decade, and 68% of people who had an advisor said they felt they were far better off than they would be had they done this themselves, and only four percent feel they would have done better being on their own."

We feel blessed to be in one of the most emotionally rewarding and impact professional services around. Providing trusted advice, developing relationships, being of great service, and adding comfort, clarity and confidence to our clients' lives is as fulfilling as it gets. There is a great need, and the demographics are going to increase the need for providing trusted advice so you can have solid growth that is safely managed, thus securing you a better future.

Reverse Dollar Cost Averaging or Disinvesting

If you have heard about and are using "dollar cost averaging" while building your asset base, you have experienced how powerful that is. It enables you buy your assets more efficiently and less expensively so your investments have the opportunity to perform well. It works like this: in good times you buy fewer shares with the same dollar amount of the world's great companies because they are dear. When times are bad, you can buy more shares with the same dollar amount. This works great during accumulation, and over the long term.

Reverse dollar cost averaging is deadly to your wealth. You are no longer adding to your portfolio. You are dis-investing. You are removing assets to fund your wants and needs. You are removing, usually, a growing amount each year to keep up with inflation. And the sequence of that removal is critical. If you remove a fixed amount or a percentage amount the sequence is important. You have little control of the time you decide to begin living off your investments. You have no control over the economy, inflation, taxes, or the markets.

So you are lucky enough to retire when the investments are rising in value, you could be set. We still have no control over the markets' timing or behavior. Unfortunately, you are unlucky enough to have to take out income when markets are declining could spell disaster. This is when you die financially before you die physically. Very painful. There are strategies and processes to avoid this.

Modern Retirement Theory

Retirement is a consumption and preservation phase of life, rather than an accumulation phase. The modern retirement theory encompasses asset management preservation and utilization strategies at the individual client level. Why is this? Put simply, retirement is an absolute, non-negotiable goal, not a relative one. Modern retirement theory attempts to mitigate income and estate taxes and is a goal-based strategy that uses a four pillar asset disbursement structure for meeting client goals. Its goal is to help clients maintain an income level to support a desired lifestyle reliably, consistently and predictably.

Modern retirement theory, which Summit Wealth practices, focuses on helping clients reach their goals in every market condition. This differs from the modern portfolio theory, which is applied during the accumulation phase. During the accumulation phase, you have a long-term time horizon. This allows you to focus on the diversification, proper asset allocation and discipline for rebalancing approach to end up with market-based returns that exceed average investor returns several fold. This cannot work in retirement, because there may not be a long-term time horizon.

In this model, there are two facts that the client cannot know: longevity and conditions with longevity. In other words, we do not know how long we will live, nor can we know how the market, inflation, economy, etc., will do during our lifetime.

Modern retirement theory, or MRT, is the brainchild of Branning and Grubbs. The four pillars of the theory are four funds in the client's circle of wealth.

These are the:

- Base fund
- Contingency fund
- Discretionary fund
- Legacy fund

Understanding each of these will help you better understand the theory as a whole.

Base Fund

The base fund is designed to provide you with your guaranteed income during retirement. This fund should provide this income in both good and poor market conditions. It should be adjusted for inflation over time, and it should remain in place for the surviving partner. Social Security can be part of this base guaranteed income. Other items that can be part of this fund include:

- Laddered CD interests
- Laddered fixed indexed annuity income
- Defined benefit pension plans
- Reverse mortgages
- Treasury inflation protected security

To best manage inflation, the income stream for this fund should be laddered. To manage credit risk, we recommend that you diversify among companies, government institutions and banks.

Contingency Fund

The contingency fund is place to help protect against unpredictable, yet highly consequential events that might occur as a result of health issues, changes in tax laws or changes in the markets.

Common tools to be used in this fund include:

- Short-term FDIC structured notes
- Laddered CDs
- Life insurance
- First aid planning

By having this fund in place, you can be certain that your income will not be destroyed by one unexpected life event.

Discretionary and Legacy Funds

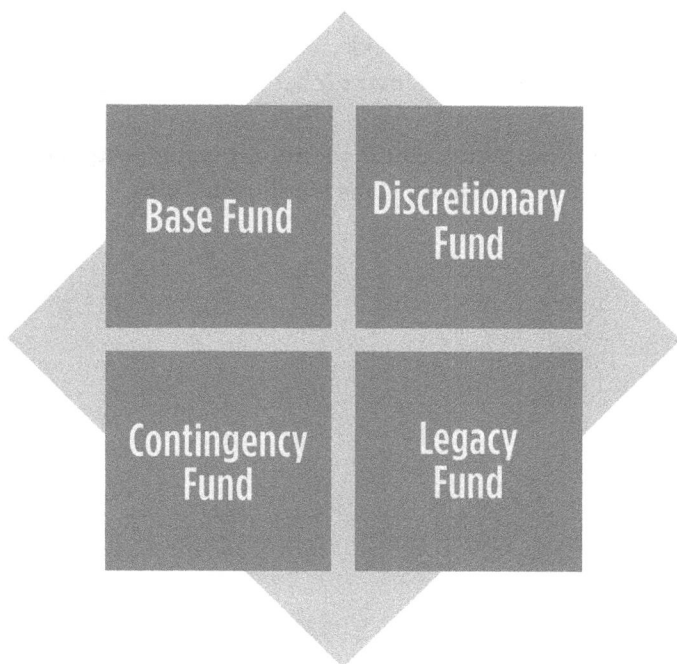

The discretionary fund, which serves as discretionary income for the retiree, has a time horizon of between 2 and 10 years. The legacy fund is what you plan to set aside for your heirs. Often, this will use trusts and other estate planning strategies to ensure that your heirs can receive what you wish to give them when you are done.

Why do we use the MRT model? It allows us to create a secure, stable and sustainable retirement for you, where income funding is not subject to the wide fluctuations of the markets, the economy, taxes and inflation, unless intentional and initiated by you.

We believe this gives you the best possible chance to live out your retirement and truly enjoy it, without worry of problems should you live a long and healthy life.

Key Takeaways

- You need to plan your distribution phase wisely
- Your distributions can be a trickle, or a torrent
- Portfolio performance and investor behavior go together, hand-in-hand
- Surveys report pre-retirement is commonly being postponed
- Modern Retirement Theory plans for all conditions

Chapter 7: Leaving Your Legacy and Being Good Stewards

"I believe that every right implies a responsibility; every opportunity, an obligation; every possession a duty."

–John D. Rockefeller, Jr.

Even though we believe that income taxes trump estate taxes in importance, we must still be good stewards and not pay more in estate taxes than is necessary. Unless you are among the few that believes the government can apportion your resources better than you can. The importance of lowering current income taxes through some of our advanced planning, and non-controversial strategies cannot be over stated. Recall the discussion regarding lost opportunity cost in Chapter 1. Having already dealt with improving your current and future income tax exposure, you have amassed substantial resources that will pass to some one or some thing. Why not control who gets what and when and how?

Estate Planning 101

When discussing distribution, you must discuss estate planning. If you have been able to accumulate a decent amount of wealth, then much of that wealth will be distributed through your estate to your heirs at some point. Proper estate planning is essential to ensure that the people you want to have receive your assets do, in fact, receive them.

Whitney Houston – What Not to Do

The premature death of Whitney Houston may serve as a concrete reminder that you need to have your estate planning set up properly through trusts, and that they need to be inspected and, at times, adjusted.

When Whitney Houston died, her will showed that her entire estate was going to her 18-year-old child as the main beneficiary. The good news is that she had a will. The bad news is that an 18-year-old is about to inherit everything from a potentially huge estate in a large lump sum. This simply does not make sense, no matter who the child is. It makes far more sense for the child to have a spendthrift clause, trustees and proper advisory to ensure that the money is used wisely. The way the will stands, Whitney's child and the estate have no protection from predators, creditors, divorce, taxation and poor investments.

Whitney also left a $1 million life insurance policy for her daughter. On paper, this seems like an adequate amount. Yet, for some, this is nowhere near enough to provide the child with a comfortable lifestyle, money for a good education and money for good financial advice.

This is why we go to great lengths to educate our clients to be certain that we are good stewards of our bounty, can leave behind the right amount for our children with boundaries, and do not have to hide our tails when explaining to the beneficiaries about how things were handled.

In the world of Hollywood and mega wealthy celebrities, too many are used to having everything done for them. Because of this, they may not know how to get quality trusted advice. A trust is no good if the trust is not funded. Estate planning attorneys need to communicate with a trusted wealth manager to ensure that the trust is not only properly created, but also properly implemented and executed.

Passing on Family Wealth Without Making Gifts

One of the goals of your estate plan should be to pass on your wealth with the minimum impact of taxes. Today, you have new wealth transfer opportunities. The Tax Relief Unemployment Insurance Reauthorization and Job Creation Act passed at the end of 2010 extended and expanded some tax cuts for the wealthy. These, unless Congress acts soon, will end at the end of 2012. So, for a limited period of time, you could have used these cuts to make a gift of up to $5,100,000 per person tax free, within certain limits.

So, was this the best option? Maybe so; maybe not. Gifting isn't for everyone, and you do not need to do this just because you can. In fact, gifting away your assets because of these expiring options could be a problem, because it could reduce your standard of living and weaken your financial flexibility.

Once you give a gift, you cannot take it back, and you lose control over that asset. Outsiders, like your heir's creditors, could end up claim that gifted money or asset. So, before you jump all over giving gifts to your heirs, make sure it is the right move.

If you decide to give, what options do you have instead of making a large gift? Can these be your alternatives if the tax credits are not extended?

First, ask yourself this question: would you be willing to reposition some of your assets to increase what you could pass on to your children? What if the following were true? There is no negative impact on your own financial security You transfer these assets after you die

You retain control over these assets while you continue to live, including our ability to recover the cost and change which family members and charities will receive those funds.

If you think that sounds like a good idea, then you are not alone. In fact, you are like the overall majority of our clients.

Here are some of the benefits we would identify:

- Predictable value
- Values not linked to market performance Liquidity
- Income tax-free payments
- Growth
- Leverage

There are many ways we can get these benefits for you. Stand by trusts using interfamily loans, private split dollar arrangements, LLCs, partnerships and freeze partnerships can all help you pass money on to your heirs with a tax break and without the risks of gifts. The choice is yours, you can be penalized by the tax code, or you can take advantage of the tax code in a legal, ethical and effective way.

We believe that you must understand the full ramification of your actions, because there are advantages and disadvantages to every step. Gifts are not always the right option, but they are not necessarily bad. You need to know the details of every choice before you.

Preparing Your Heirs

One of the problems with leaving your wealth to those behind you is the risk of giving young people too much, too soon, particularly if you leave behind your wealth prematurely. We have seen time and time again how the wealth our clients worked hard to attain is squandered by immature, uneducated heirs. That is why part of our estate planning services includes building relationships with your beneficiaries so we can help them make the most of their potential inheritance.

We will help them remember these four things:

- The importance of diversifying so their future isn't wedded to any particular company, style, manager or asset class.
- The fact that because they have already gotten the windfall, there's no reason to take on extra risks to try and hit another homerun.

After receiving an inheritance, base hits and singles are the best choice.

- Even with a sizeable investment, they do need a plan. An investment plan, a financial plan, an income plan, an asset protection plan and an estate plan are all vital. Without them, things can go wrong in a big way, real fast.
- They should not act too quickly. Many mistakes are made in the first few months after a windfall inheritance. Heirs should receive some education so they're not surprised about a potential sudden windfall and, perhaps, the education ought to include the charitable intent of the creator of the wealth.

Of course, we do not keep your heirs from having a little fun with their inheritance, but we believe that fun should be in moderation, so they can enjoy the destination as well as the journey. Prudence is the watchword. They need to seek solid growth that is safely managed. This is only possible through trusted advice from a wealth management professional. Even in cases of a windfall, heirs need to make great decisions.

Charitable Giving

Many of our clients feel blessed to be as financially secure as they are, and they want to do something to give to others, to share in their blessings, either during their lifetimes or after their deaths. Many tax benefits make charitable giving appealing, but it must be done right for you to benefit.

We work closely with tax exempt, charitable organizations to help their donors help them. This is not "donor motivation". This is not donor marketing.

On the contrary, "Giving Until it Hurts No Longer Applies." Using simple and inexpensive strategies, you can be in a better position, while giving more. The reason you may not be doing this harks back to our introductory discussions about myths and misconceptions. The biggest one being the fallacy that "I have a guy" who handles this; whether it is the accountant, the attorney, or the financial advisor.

Unfortunately, no one is really taking care of the positioning. Some of the strategies are so inexpensive, that it is not worth their while to get involved in it. But you can give more and more easily, simply by identifying the sources of wealth erosion and re-positioning your assets. The world of private wealth management is highly complex and complicated and regulated one. It requires close collaboration and integration with your accountant, your attorney, your insurances and your finances. Here are some thoughts.

Make the Most of Your Charitable Gifts

In theory, giving to charity should be simple. You choose a charity, get some money and give it to them. However, making the most of your charitable gifts so you get the maximum tax benefit is complicated. That is why you need to seek trusted advice before you start giving away your money.

We understand that charitable giving is important to you, but so is protecting your wealth. We want to help you do both. Let's start by defining charitable gifting. This is giving to causes that are meaningful to you, because you want to help others. Members of a church may tithe, and this is charitable giving. Others may donate to the Salvation Army, and this would also qualify.

America is the most charitable country on earth, and has been even before the tax code was created in 1913. Yet, there are still incentives for charity within the tax code, and many of them are complicated and inefficient. That's why charitable giving is much more complex than it should be!

It's important to understand the different areas in which one can gift charitably.

The most common areas are:

- Religious institutions
- Educational institutions
- Healthcare institutions
- Social service institutions
- Arts institutions

Once you find a charity you are passionate about, you have two basic ways to contribute. One is what we like to call "checkbook gifting." This is where you may write a check for a sizeable amount towards the charitable organization. The other is leaving a charitable legacy. This could be a deferment of $50,000 to spread over five years, or a $250,000 one-time gift followed by $50,000 a year after that. These types of ongoing gifts can be more meaningful to your chosen organization because they represent ongoing income.

So, now that we know what charitable gifting is, how can we make sure that it is the most effective? First, let's discuss whether or not your large gift is eligible for a private foundation or a donor advised fund. A private foundation requires about $30 million to be meaningful, and this is out of the question for most of our clients. Since we serve the "middle class millionaire," the donor advised fund (DAF) is typically a better option. These are inexpensive and can be established immediately, whereas private foundations have large legal and other fees, and they can take weeks or even months to create.

Startup cost and time are only the first difference between these two types of gifts. They also have tax deduction limit differentials. You can deduct 50% off of your adjusted gross income in a DAF compared to only 30% for a private foundation. There are tax deduction limits for stock or real property as well, and you can deduct 30% in a DAF versus only 20% in a private foundation. So, deduction potential is higher with a DAF.

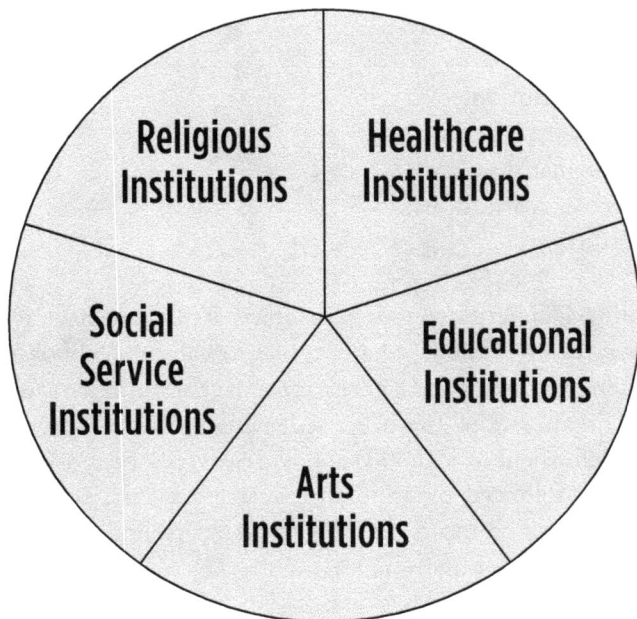

Isn't it great when deciding who to give to is the hardest part?

The valuation of the gifts is also different. In a DAF, the gift is valued at fair market value. Private foundations receive fair market value for publicly traded securities only, and are valued on a cash basis for other gifts.

Privacy is yet another difference. Donor advised funds can have anonymous donors, if you desire. Private foundations are required to provide detailed annual statements on grants, fees, staff and salaries, and these are made public, so anonymity is virtually impossible.

These two types of gifts have a difference in a required payout. If you chose DAF, you have no required payout. Private foundations, however, must pay out five percent of their net assets annually. Also, of the two funds, only private foundations pay excise taxes, which are between one and two percent on annual net investment income.

In light of these differences, it is easy to see why a DAF makes the most sense for the majority of our clients who do not have the amount to gift that would cover all of these expenses and taxes.

Once you choose a type of charitable gifting structure, you need to maximize the impact of your contributions.

Here are five ways you can do so:

- You can identify like-minded charitable people and pool your charitable resources to make a very large meaningful gift together
- You can benefit by working your gifting into your estate plan
- You can give away highly appreciated assets
- You can spread your gifting over time or gift it all at once as the asset accumulates
- You can sit on the boards or give your time to the board of the charity you choose.

Which of these is the best? The answer will depend on many factors, but you can easily make the decision with the help of trusted advice.

As you work with non-profits, you will likely find that one of the more difficult things in the non-profit world is board governance. Sadly, the people who sit on the board of your chosen organization may not share your ideals. In fact, in some instances they may not be trying to further what is good for the community or the charity.

To ensure that the charity is fulfilling the goals you hope to accomplish with your gift, consider sitting on a board, and take the time to read the articles of incorporation and bylaws of the organization. Analyze financial statements to ensure that your goals are being put into play. If you need help in that area, or do not have the desire or skill set to analyze these documents yourself, contact our charitable planning department for help. our experts can dissect these documents and help you ensure that the charity is doing what you want it to do with the money you gave.

There is a saying in the non-profit world that their best donors give their time, talent, and treasure. All three things are what make a successful charity. Charitable gifting is one of the qualities that make this country great. Make sure that you plan properly in order to maximize the impact of your contributions, not just on your own estate but also on the charities to which you contribute.

When Philanthropy Goes Wrong

If you give while you live, you can be certain that your funds are supporting causes you believe in. This is becoming one of the most important presets of philanthropy. Today's donors are demanding accountability for the funds they give.

Do you remember the case where the Bass brothers sent a $1 million gift to Yale, only to sue them for a refund later because the school did not use the money as they saw fit? Or what about the $100 million settlement Princeton made to the Robertson Foundation in 2008? When we set up a foundation to dribble its funds in perpetuity, there's a high risk it will eventually drift into projects the donor did not believe in. Since the donor is no longer living, he or she cannot oversee the fund and ensure it is doing the intended task.

Some foundation founders of the past were happy to let others make the decisions for them. John Dean McArthur of the Epitomes Foundation told his trustees, "I'll make the money. You people after I'm dead will have to learn how to spend it." The Ford Foundation followed a similar path. Henry Ford I once said, "I do not believe in giving folks things. I do believe in giving them a chance to make things for themselves." Yet, he left no instructions of the purposes of the Ford Foundation. Mismanagement of the fund led to the resignation of Henry Ford II from the Board of the Foundation in 1977. Other foundations have been similarly mismanaged, as trustees and boards have a selfish interest in perpetuating the fund to ensure their ongoing salaries, even if the creator's goals are no longer being met. This is philanthropy gone badly.

New fund creators have learned from these mistakes and are making changes in the structure of their foundations. For example, the newest and largest foundation is the Bill and Melinda Gates Foundation. It was designed to close 75 years after the couple's death. This has several effects. First, a greater amount of money can be concentrated toward achieving the Foundation's goals. Second, the Foundation's board members no longer have a selfish reason in perpetuating that foundation.

Of course, none of us have the hundreds of millions of dollars of the Bill Gates foundation. The average private foundation is slightly less than half a million dollars in the United States, due to income tax and estate tax laws. There may even be better ways for you to give your charitable gift then through a foundation. Regardless, if you are giving money to a charity, you need to clearly define your purpose.

You can do this by:

- Defining your mission. Write it down so you have it clearly spelled out.
- Choosing trustees and staff who share your fundamental principles.
- Separating your philanthropic interests from your interests in maintaining control of your estate.
- Giving generously while you're alive in a way that you can oversee and guide.
- Creating strong procedures for electing future trustees who share your principles, should you decide to establish a foundation that extends beyond 75 years, making respect for donor intent part of their fiduciary duty.

Remember, it is your money, and you should have a say in how it is spent, even when you give it to charity. By carefully setting up the structure of your gift, you can avoid having your money fall into the hands of self-serving trustees long after you are gone.

Key Takeaways

- Estate plans must be properly created *and* executed
- Giving heirs too much, too soon can be a critical mistake
- "Giving until it hurts" no longer applies
- Most people assume their "guy" is taking care of "it"
- There are plenty of donor options that protect your anonymity

Chapter 8: Reclaiming the Future

"Education is an ornament in prosperity and a refuge in adversity."
—Aristotle

Americans are about to face one of the most pronounced retirement income challenges in history. First, they'll no longer be able to count on once reliable sources of retirement income, such as defined benefit plans. Second, increasing longevity will bring a real risk of outliving retirement savings. Finally, increased personal responsibility for retirement savings will make retirees more vulnerable to market turbulence. These three factors could serious impact America's, and your, retirement preparedness.

In May of 2010, Larson Research and Strategy Consulting and DSS Research concluded a nationwide online survey of 3,257 US adults between the ages of 44 and 75. The margin for error for this total sample was plus or minus 1.7%. It revealed several interesting things:

- Many Americans believe there is a retirement crisis, and that they are unprepared
- We have five distinct financial personalities
- Americans fear outliving their money more than they fear death
- The economic downturn was a big wake-up call
- Annuity-like solutions are gaining relevance and appeal, and probably should be given a better look

Now let us take a closer look at these. In the survey, an overwhelming 92% of respondents indicated they were concerned about the retirement crisis. This is substantial, and it points to just how scared we all are.

In light of this fear, people fall into five distinct personalities. These are:

- Overwhelmed – These individuals do not know what to do with their fear
- Iconic – These individuals feel they are well prepared for the future and have a strong belief in the American Dream
- Resilient – These individuals have a take charge attitude, have planned ahead, but plan to work a little harder to make up for the pending problems.
- Distracted – These individuals have seen their net worth drop, but they have done nothing about it.
- Savvy – These individuals are already living comfortably in retirement or have made the changes necessary to retire comfortably. They are properly advised and financially independent.

For those who reported that they fear running out of money more than death, the majority (63%) were between the ages of 40 and 49. Of those, 83% had dependents. Many investors are expecting to postpone their retirement, and 401(k) plan participants are asking for more employer help than ever before. This fear is causing many Americans to state their risk tolerance is lower. In July 2012, a report from Reuters indicated that Americans are losing sleep over their retirement problems, and half reported having a diminished appetite.

What are we worried about? We are worried about maintaining our lifestyles while supporting ourselves and our extended families, dealing with rising healthcare costs and having something left to leave behind.

As they went into the economic downturn, the people surveyed indicated it served as a wakeup call. Close to half said they found ways to cut their daily expenses and that they're more engaged financially, while almost 25% said they were watching or reading more financial news. Another 15% reported paying greater attention to fine print, and 14% started reading financial statements a lot more closely.

Finally, the report showed that annuity-like solutions are gaining relevance and appeal. Nearly 70% of the people surveyed said they prefer a product that was guaranteed not to lose value, while only 31% chose a product whose goal was providing a high rate of return. An overwhelming 80% of people surveyed preferred a product with a four percent return and a guarantee against losing value over a product with eight percent return and vulnerability to market downturns.

Yet, there are substantial misconceptions about this, because a surprising 54% of respondents expressed distaste for the word "annuity," even after describing an annuity-like product as their ideal financial vehicle. Why is this? Further answers may show some insight. After all, 25% of those who responded formed their opinion of annuities based on products they saw or used more than 20 years ago. A full 64% admit they have not researched annuities in the years since.

Could annuities be the key to reclaiming the future? Again, we come back to the same answer. There is no single tool that is the answer to our current financial mess. It is a whole toolbox that provides the solution. With a diversified portfolio, which may include some annuities or similar products with guaranteed returns, you can weather this financial mess and come out with plenty of income to live out your retirement comfortably.

The Future Is Bright

There are two trillion reasons to consider the future to be bright. Not too long ago, corporate America's cash pile had hit its highest level in fifty-one years, representing 7.5% of all corporate assets. The actual number is two trillion dollars. That's the highest percent of all corporate assets. This two trillion dollar cash buildup shows the deep caution many companies are feeling about investing in expansion while the economic recovery remains painfully slow. It shows how battered household finances, high unemployment and federal debt continue to limit consumers' ability to spend.

Now, for companies, this cash buildup has a big downside. They see little return for their money because interest rates are so low. Yet, there is a bright side to this. The Federal Reserve data shows that the net worth of US households actually increased to 53 trillion dollars in the third quarter of 2010. This is an astoundingly large number, even in an economically "difficult" time. The markets defy the Feds bond buying push. Many fear that this increased push for bonds whips inflation to dangerous levels. Currently, the 10-year Treasury is sitting at around three percent, while the 30-year Treasury sits slightly above a four percent rate of return.

What are all of these figures telling us? Truthfully, as with other predictors, no one really knows. What we do know is that there is capital sitting on the sidelines waiting to be deployed. So, we can say, the future is bright.

Now, does this mean stocks will rise, fall or stay the same? Again, nobody knows. Also, nobody knows when, by how much or for how long this money could make a difference. We believe the future is bright, but we also understand that we do not quite know how bright or how to best make use of this fact. We have no control over the markets, the economy, inflation or taxes, but we do have control over what we do with your portfolio. That is why we are going to push for a prudently invested, diversified, properly allocated and properly rebalanced portfolio. Then, you will be poised to jump when this bright future starts to materialize.

There Is Hope!

My friend, Don Blanton, once remarked, "If what you thought to be true turned not to be true, when would you want to know? And more importantly, what would you do about it?" There is no denying we face uncertain economic times in some ways, but we feel it is important for you to remember that this is not the first time things have gotten difficult. It is not the end of the world. Help is available, and that help comes in the form of trusted financial advice from a trustworthy advisor.

We stress, we agonize, we fear, and we react. Yet, the sky has refused to fall. We have feared this for millennia. We rationalize by using the most dangerous four words in the English language: "this time is different". Well this time is NOT different. It has never been different. Things have been worse, and they may worsen further. Even three years after the great recession was declared officially over, unemployment remains high and there may be worry about a new recession or depression or disinflation or deflation or massive inflation. And then we've got economic and political and tax policies to deal with.

The facts, however, paint a better picture. This does not mean we make light of the intense, deep problems we face in our un-employment, our national debt and the possibly impending "tax-armageddon", inflation, our political polarization, our government involvement in all things, and more.

Yet, could there be a coming boom in America? Get ready for it. We will lay out the facts shortly. This year we worried about the election as apocalypse. Is it merely the *disaster du jour*? Regarding this political season, please refer to the vitriol of Jefferson vs. Adams. And who was it that said "the only thing new in this world is the history we don't know"?

While you have read in these pages that "luck is not a good strategy", perhaps we must all keep in mind that "dread is not an investment policy" either.

We often say, "protect principal." Should we not really say, "preserve purchasing power" instead? They are very different, requiring very different strategies. How many of us have made financial decisions that resulted in an unexpected or disappointing outcome? It is not because we are stupid, illogical, and irrational.

Could it not be that we based those decisions on missing facts, misinformation, myths, or misconceptions? Would you not agree that it is important to know the critical, must-know facts prior to making those decisions?

Statistics show, surveys support, and our experience with people prior to becoming our clients confirms that too many people experience mistakes that cost very much money, or could cause a big problem in the future.

Providing those facts, de-bunking those myths and misconceptions is paramount to our clients. Bringing that clarity is what we do -- along with applying a disciplined, evidence-based approach to protect, and preserve you hard-earned wealth.

Firms like ours, fiduciaries, do not make you wealthy. We prevent your large fortune from becoming a small one. Finding the money you may not even have known you were losing, and bringing that money back to you, is one very important way we do that. Employing the must-know facts brings a sense of comfort and confidence in the decisions and the future, our clients tell us.

It empowers a strong sense of control. And "empowering full financial health" is our stated mission. We believe this will improve the world, one investor at a time.

We provide the clarity, so you can have the comfort, have the confidence, to take back, and feel in, control again. We do not really care where the markets (or for that matter, the economy, taxes, or inflation) are going. We have no control over their direction, nor their duration.

We care about how *you* are doing. It is not about prediction. It is about perspective. We keep talking about rational optimism. We keep talking about how it's too early to count America down. We talk about demographics, and how we are demographically positioned to be the Western Civilization growth engine, but what we have not talked about are the industry applications that are out there.

Here are the facts we promised. This should help the perspective. Because, it truly is not the end of world.

One year after the ratings agencies stripped America of its AAA credit rating, mortgage rates have dropped to record lows, yields on Treasuries have plummeted, and the U.S. stock market has sky-rocketed. Could this mean an impending deflation? Are we likely to become to Japan? Not likely. See our previous article "We are not Japan."

True, the dollar is now only worth some 18 cents compared to 1954, representing a 5-plus-fold decline. Yet our stock markets have increased some 15-fold in that same time period. If we adjust for inflation, is that not a 3-fold increase?

OK, that is a very long period. What about the last 10 years, you may rightly ask? True our stock market was practically flat. Yet, many diversified, and rebalanced portfolios also are up over significantly in the last 10 years.

The best of times tend to follow the worst of times. How about an abiding faith in the historical record, in the greatness of the free markets, in America, in ourselves? A $15 trillion U.S. economy does not, cannot implode, or completely disappear. People still have to buy food, go to work, buy transportation, use computers...And only two generations ago, in today's dollars, the total economy was one seventh. The same for the $13 Trillion Eurozone economy.

As of the time of this writing, we are in the middle of the "cheap revolution." Everything is less expensive. (So we buy more of it— more house, more car, more education, more eating out, etc.) And everything is getting better. Transportation cost, food costs, housing costs, entertainment costs, computers, televisions, communications are lower as a percentage of our overall economy.

Even our poor are relatively wealthy, with a greater living standard than the Eurozone's middle class. Our poor have indoor plumbing and air conditioning, cell phones, large screen televisions and cable, education, health care access, and more. They live better than many of the wealthy of by-gone eras.

And who could have foreseen that we'd be in a burst of growth with wealth creation as big as any in living memory. We'll list here, just a few of them:

1. NanoCulture – one of the truths of tech is that revolutions take longer than predicted. But they arrive sooner than we are prepared for them. And that may be the case with nanotechnology, the hot new science story of a decade ago. Nanotech is now coming into its own with breakthrough medicines, genetic research, new materials, such as graphene, a latis-sheet form of carbon used for everything from filters to computer chips. Molecular electronics, which allows for extreme miniaturization with super small censors and other devices. Quantum computing – and more.

1. What about the cloud crowd? - In the world of information technology, the big story these days is the shift of data management from in-house computing centers to rented, easily scalable computing and storage from anonymous servers located somewhere out in the Internet. Big data is the application of all this new computing power. And big data offers measuring precision in science, business, medicine, and in almost every other sector never before possible. Over the next few years it will spread across every industry and scientific discipline.

3. Printing dreams – three dimensional printing is manufacturing technology that creates specific objects from buildings to machine components and even human organs by laying down layers of material or carving away from a block of existing material. Even

though it's been around for several years, it soon will influence everyday life. New materials; such as, molten polymers and metal powders and highly focused lasers and increasingly, nanotech and 3-D printing is an incredibly powerful design and modeling tool. We can already find hundreds of consumer products, from furniture to jewelry created with 3-D printing. There will be gears and motors and industry components. Imagine the future with a 3-D printer in your own home on your desk.

4. Hand-held diplomas. The discrepancy between the cost of university tuition and the return on investment for most students grows every year. Virtual courses on laptops, smart phones, and tablets, is a shift that's already beginning to transform higher education and bring in a host of new competitors.

5. Self health. Examples include eye triage and other applications to find a nearby health provider while blood tests for diabetics can connect iPhone and users to sync and manage information from test readings.

This stuff is not only on the way, it's already here. Together these trends offer a potential for another golden era. Just because it appears the car is heading toward the cliff, does not mean we will not take our foot off the gas, apply the brakes, turn away from the cliff, run out gas, or something else. Take heart, a better world awaits us.

Our Predictions

We can guaranty where the markets, the economy, taxes and inflation are going. They will either go up, down, or sideways.

Unfortunately, we do not know when, by how much, or for how long. This is not meant to be cute or cynical. It is meant to help you get and remain prepared for all eventualities. True, using this approach you will not make a killing in the good times, and you will not get killed by bad the events. We have said time and time again that no one can know the future. This remains true. Yet, with the help of history, we can make informed predictions. Will they come true? Who knows, but they are made with the basis of historical evidence.

Which direction will the markets go?

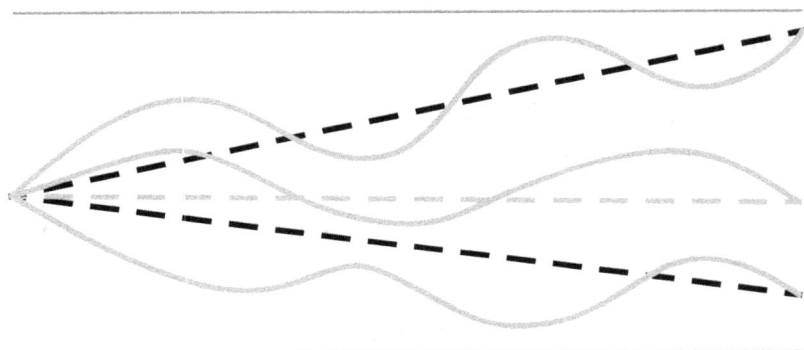

The Next Several Years

Today's biggest investment fear boils down to one thing: recession. We have faced one, and some believe we will face a second. While there's no guarantee that there won't be a double dip, we do know with certainty that another recession now would be unprecedented. According to Tim Fisher in Forbes, we have never had a recession after the traditional leading economic indicator index has been high and rising for five months. Yet, that is what is happening today on an absolute, year after year basis.

Many "gurus" liked to compare 2011 with what was happening in 2007 through 2009. Back then, the leading economic index had been falling for three years, which is not the case today. Also, take a look at the yield curve. This leading economic indicator is one that bond investors watch closely because it illustrates the spread or the difference between the long-term interest rate and the short-term interest rate. It is always been low, but just before a recession it tends to be negative. In 2007, it was negative. Yet, more recently, the spread is 2.2%. While not high, this is not negative either.

Since World War II, we have not experienced a recession until after corporate profits per employee had declined for at least six months. Currently, just the opposite is happening. This indicator is continuing to rise. So, those pundits pounding the table claiming that job growth must come before economic growth tend to ignore the statistical evidence. Profitability always comes first.

All of these indicators show that it is highly unlikely that we will have another recession just around the corner. We're also unlikely to have a major bear market in the next 15 months. Of course, it could happen, but history seems to indicate that it is not likely.

The media and market watchers are obsessing over whether the S&P 500 was down 19% versus, say, 25% for the NASDAQ. Swinging down more than 20% will spark headlines claiming we are in a full fledged and utterly bear market, but this has little real meaning. The markets are volatile and they fluctuate daily. Instead of focusing on this, focus on the world's greatest companies and how well they will do, and keep your mind on how well they will do when the market starts to improve.

"Gloom and doomers" are a dime a dozen. It is no different now than it was in 2007 or back in the 1980s. Avoid the problems we have discussed, such as gambling and speculating, market timing and stock picking, and stay prudently invested with proper allocation.

Remember, when you are dealing with your finances, it is wise to stay conservative. The only ones who get rich in the stock market are the fund managers. You are already rich, so stop making this your focus. Instead, make your focus to stay rich and never get poor. This is what we will do for you.

Why We Are Hopeful

We have said it several times, but we are very hopeful about the current economic state of affairs. Yes, we see the same depressing stories you do, and we understand why you do not feel confident. There are government reports that the poverty rate is increasing. There are media stories about the pending inflation problem and the spiraling Eurozone. The local news talks about how there are few jobs for young people and the consumer price index could be increasing.

Why should we be hopeful about the future? Simple. It is very difficult to hold America down. Why would we want to bet on that? People often perform best with their backs to the wall. People adapt, business evolves and the US economy always finds a way. As one of the two countries in the world that are purpose built, this is the number one country where people still are banging on the door to get in. People want what America offers. It is also the number one country to find safe havens for investments. It is the number one country for rules of law and property rights. The bottom line is, it is the best country to live and invest in.

Because of this, our population will grow. In fact, over the next 40 years, it is expected to grow by another 100 million. Technology is increasing at an accelerating pace. Information is more readily available, and is increasing at astronomical rates.

Sure, the poverty rate may be increasing, but our poor now live better than the typical European middle class. To be poor in this country can mean air conditioning, cell phones, cable TV, free healthcare, free food, free schooling, free transportation and a roof over your head. It is wonderful how far our standard of living has increased, and to think that it won't increase in the future is not logical. That is why we are so optimistic, and we are ready to help you jump into this positive future with both feet, making great decisions to capitalize on each and every investment you make.

Key Takeaways

- Retiring Americans are fearful
- No single tool will work for all situations; however, each tool has a use if applied properly
- This time is not different; this time is *never* different
- Protect your purchasing power
- America is innovating – our future is bright

Chapter 9: Back in Control

"Fiduciaries and other investors are confronted with potent evidence that the application of expertise, investigation, and diligence in effort to "beat the market' ordinarily promises little or no payoff, or even a negative payoff, after taking account of research and transaction costs."
–The American Law Institute-*Third Restatement of the Law, Trust,*
Prudent Investor Rule

By now you have seen that by eliminating the myths, mis-information, and misconceptions, and by identifying the missing information, you can be empowered to make great financial decisions with clarity, and eliminate the unexpected results, and the disappointments. By identifying and addressing phantom income tax, the Dalbar gap, inflation, qualified health care riders, private capital reserve strategies, and many others, you no longer have to be a statistic. When you take the next industry survey, you now may be a positive outlier with clarity and confidence in the future. This should give you further comfort in the decision making process, and confidence to really know the risks, alternatives, benefits, and likely outcomes of an evidence-based process. Thus, you get to regain and to feel in control once again.

Likewise, you have seen how having the complete and correct information can empower to you to greater success and control in your future. You can see that having uncommon income and assets requires uncommon advice. You can see how finding the money is critical. You can see how having a thorough and simple discovery process can bring you greater clarity and confidence. You can see that myths and misconceptions, missing or mis-information can cost you money now or cause a big problem in the future. You can see that having that power can be comforting.

It can help you avoid the losses, which is more powerful than picking the winners. That consistent excellence out-performs occasional brilliance. And that solid growth, safely managed through trusted advice is key to creating that better future. It is our mission to empower you to full financial health. This will improve the world, one investor at a time. Beginning with you.

According to PrivateWealthManagement.com's reported survey results, three out of four clients want true wealth management, not just investment advice. Yet only 6% of firms deliver that. The reasons: it is difficult to provide true wealth management; it is time consuming to provide true wealth management; it requires expertise many do not have to provide true wealth management.

To be a true wealth manager requires us to employ the proper discovery methodologies; to utilize solutions that are outside of mere investment consulting, including maximizing charitable giving, preserving wealth, taking care of your family when you are no longer able to, protecting assets from creditors and predators and bad actors, and bringing world class service to it all. How does it go, "if all you have is a hammer, everything looks like a nail?" You are not all alike. We should not rely on only one tactic or tool. So we have one abiding philosophy, a consistent process to discover your needs, and apply the appropriate solutions, and a commitment to place your interests ahead of our own, always and everywhere.

If you have not heard some of these concepts or risks or costs before reading this book, ask yourself -- why? Are they not important to you? Is it because you are not accessing the expertise? Or is it because there may be a conflict of interest? And which is worse? At the risk of getting to cliche-ish, "change is difficult; that is why coins are made from metal."

We hope that through gaining a closer look at our investment strategies and philosophies, we have shown you how we are different than other financial advisors and brokerage firms. With our four-step approach to investing and our radical idea that it is about the process, not the product, we are able to offer reliable, repeatable, and steady growth on your investments. Solid growth that is safely managed. If you are serious about your money and protecting your lifestyle, then you want the team at Summit Wealth on your side, creating a custom plan to help you reach your investment goals.

We understand that your goals are not the same as the last client we saw. Everyone is different. Everyone's situation is different. That is why our thorough internal discovery process will analyze your situation carefully, so we can provide an effective solution for your needs. Our goal is to give you all of the information you need to make an evidence-based decision.

If that sounds refreshing to you, then contact us at Summit Wealth today to set up your complimentary, simple, three step RITE Financial Diagnosis. The three diagnostic steps include evaluations for Risk, Income and True Market Investments Analysis, and Tax optimization. If you are eligible a fourth step for Estate planning analysis is necessary. Let us help you find the ways you could be losing valuable funds while giving you strategies to increase your financial success.

Let us help you to achieve clarity of purpose and understanding of the ramifications of your decision making. We will help you regain your comfort with your situation, regain confidence in the future for you and your loved ones, and ultimately, regain control. With Summit Wealth, you can make great decisions.

Key Takeaways
- Proper discovery is critical to gaining clarity and creating a plan that meets your needs and expectations
- Complete and accurate information empowers you

- Three out of four financial clients desire true wealth management services
- More reliable and repeatable results are available

Epilogue

Happy with This Book?

Consider Introducing These Concepts

First, please share this book with those important to you.

If you are already a Summit Wealth client, you are happy with how we have helped you stabilize your portfolio, so please consider introducing your friends and family to us. The people you care about are going to go somewhere for their financial help. It make sense for you to introduce these people to someone you know, like and trust, yes?

We employ and enjoy a relationship model. You and any family or friends you refer to us will build a relationship with your advisor, and our team. Our professionals will know what you like to talk about and develop a chemistry with you. We work hard to keep our fees low, find money you may be losing, and help you invest that money to bring long-term success. We keep your privacy at the forefront of all of our decision-making. Our team treats your assets as if they were our own. As you have already gathered, we eat our own cooking. The recommendations and solutions we discuss in this book, we utilize ourselves.

You already benefit from all that Summit offers. Now, you are empowered to help those that you care about: introduce them to us. If you do, we will continue to earn the trust and confidence you have placed in our team. Thank you for your kind introduction and referral. Simply tell those you care about, "these are the people I like and trust" when you hand them this book. These are the people I like and trust.

Acknowledgements

As CEO and Managing Director of Summit Wealth Partners, I have the privilege of working with some of the finest financial minds and institutions this industry has to offer. Although my name appears as the author, this book would not have been possible without the contributions of many individuals.

My deepest gratitude goes to my partners Chad Warrick, Senior Wealth Advisor and Chief Investment Officer, as well as Jason Print, CFP®, Senior Wealth Advisor. Both are consummate professionals and terrific men. I am proud to call them my partners and enjoy working with them in the spirit of collaboration on behalf of our firm.

Thank you also to: Roccy M. DeFrancesco, Jr., JD, CWPP™, CAPP™, CMP™, founder of The Wealth Preservation Institute, the creator of the Certified Wealth Preservation Planner (CWPP™), Certified Asset Protection Planner (CAPP™), Certified Medicaid Planner (CMP™) designations and the co-founder of the Asset Protection Society; Don Blanton, president and founder of MoneyTrax and The Circle of Wealth System®, for which I am a Master Mentor; Terry O'Brien, owner First Benefits Group, Inc. and Kevin Fink from Houston, TX for his "Circle of Knowledge" concept; Mark Matson, founder and CEO of Matson Money, Inc., a Cincinnati-based investment advisor firm; Nick Murray, the 2007 recipient of the Malcolm S. Forbes Public Awareness Award for Excellence in Advancing Financial Understanding; Bill Johnson, president of Windows of Opportunity, a 20 year multi-million dollar financial services provider, coach and consultant. DFA Dimensional Funds Advisors, an investment firm using modeling based on the science of capital markets; and Advisors Excel Advisors, an independently owned insurance marketing organization (IMO) focused on helping independent advisors.

My appreciation goes to members of my team, beginning with Kyle Johnson for spearheading this project, for his patience and perseverance; to Ed Ventiera and his hours of research and organization of the manuscript; and to Vicki Brodnax for her attention to detail and editing skills.

And finally, to my wife Swantje, who is my biggest fan and chief critic, thank you for your endless support and for making our lives better.

About the Author

Mitch Levin, MD, CWPP, CAPP *The Financial Physician™*

Mitch Levin, MD, CWPP, CAPP, The Financial Physician™ graduated from Beloit College with a degree in English Literature in 1976. Afterwards, went to work in the Harvard Graduate School department of surgery computer labs under the Chief of Surgery, then attended SUNY Stony Brook School of Medicine, where he developed his interest in financial matters and was instrumental in setting up, what may be the first and completely student-financed long-term endowment campaign through insurance and derivative products.

In the early 2000s, Dr. Levin retired from active practice of medicine to devote himself to philanthropic endeavors and to his family. It was during this period, he became increasing interested in financial matters and investment. Ultimately, this led him to begin a new career in the field of wealth management and he became "The Financial Physician™" and CEO of Summit Wealth partners, Inc.

Dr. Levin is certified in Wealth Preservation Planning and Asset Protection Planning and is an "AA" rated Florida State Representative of the Asset Protection Society. He is a two-time national best-selling author, trusted advisor and accomplished public speaker.

His published works include a multitude of professional articles and papers, as well as the books *Power Principles for Success; How Elite Advisors GROW!; Shift Happens; Smart Choices for Serious Money;* and *Cover Your Assets: How to Build, Protect and Maintain Your Own Financial Fortress; Under the Radar;* and *The Science of Successful Investing Made Simple.*

You may contact Dr. Levin at *mlevin@mysummitwealth.com* .